THE EXPECTANT KNITTER

THE EXPECTANT KNITTER

30 Designs for Baby and Your Growing Family

MARIE CONNOLLY

PHOTOGRAPHY BY JOE SHYMANSKI

Technical Illustrations by Peggy Greig
Illustrations by Kim Bartko

POTTER CRAFT

NEW YORK

The author and publisher would like to thank the Craft Yarn Council of America for providing the yarn weight standards and accompanying icons used in this book. For more information, please visit www.YarnStandards.com.

Copyright © 2008 by Marie Connolly

Published in the United States by Potter Craft, an imprint of the Crown Publishing Group, a division of Random House, Inc., New York.
www.clarksonpotter.com
www.pottercraft.com

POTTER CRAFT and colophon is a registered trademark of Random House, Inc.

Library of Congress Cataloging-in-Publication Data

Connolly, Marie.
The expectant knitter : 30 designs for baby and your growing family / by Marie Connolly. -- 1st ed.
     p.   cm.
Includes index.
ISBN 978-0-307-40660-6
1. Knitting—Patterns.   2. Infants' clothing.   I. Title.
     TT825.C656   2008
   746.43'2041—dc22   2008003929

ISBN 978-0-307-40660-6

Printed in China

Design by Kim Bartko
Photography by Joe Shymanski

13 5 7 9 10 8 6 4 2

First Edition

This book is dedicated to my family:
Nora, Cole, Alan, and Zuzu.
Thanks for all your help, support, and love
throughout this project and every day.

My Inspiration

I MET MY KNITTING MUSE SEVEN YEARS AGO. It happened on May 19 to be exact. Her name is Nora, and she is my daughter. She inspired me to start knitting again. Knitting for Nora became an obsession. I later turned that obsession into a career when I opened my first store in Washington, DC. As the owner of three yarn stores, I now knit every day. You name it, I've either knit it or helped someone knit it. At the end of the day, my favorite project is always the one I'm working on for my muse.

Is it possible to have two muses? In early 2006, I learned that I was pregnant with my second child. I was so excited. I would have another opportunity to knit wee things. And this time, it would be for a boy. I selected soft, luxurious fibers in brilliant colors and started knitting the baby essentials—socks, hats, sweaters, and pants. As the months passed, my enthusiasm and belly grew. So did my cache of knitting projects, which included blankets, toys, and sweaters for the new big sister and even our dog.

Explore this book and the patterns enclosed, which have been lovingly tested and knit for my children, family, and friends. I included my favorite patterns in this book to provide you

with a wonderful collection of hand-knits for the new baby, nursery, and family. I hope you find your muse and that these projects inspire your creative energies.

I designed this book to serve as a guide through pregnancy. It includes health, diet, and knitting suggestions for the next forty weeks. Chapters, organized by trimester, include strategies for preparing your family members and pets for the new arrival, baby gear and diaper options, and, of course, knitting projects. The projects are tailored to the moods and realities of each trimester, as well.

Congratulations, and good luck during your pregnancy!

Sizing Guide

WHAT SIZE TO KNIT? Babies grow at different rates. Except for the swaddled infant Aria, the babies photographed in the book—Cole, Eleanor, and Elise—were all born days apart in December 2006. It was fun to see how different each was. Elise is delicate, while Cole is somewhat of a bruiser. When selecting a size, it is best to measure the recipient, then knit the size that would be closest to that measurement. Because babies seem to grow overnight, don't be surprised that sometimes the sweater knit for one baby may not fit when finished, but hopefully, another baby will enjoy it.

For the patterns in this book I used measurements from the Standards and Guidelines for Crochet and Knitting as compiled by the Craft Yarn Council of America:

0–6 MONTHS: chest 20" (51cm); head 13½" (34.5cm); waist 16" (41cm)

12 MONTHS: chest 22" (56cm); head 15½" (39.5cm); waist 17½" (44.5cm)

18 MONTHS: chest 25" (63.5cm); head 18½" (47 cm); waist 18½" (47cm)

24 MONTHS: chest 26" (66cm); head 20" (51cm); waist 20½" (52cm)

Baby Dreams

EVEN BEFORE YOU'RE OFFICIALLY PREGNANT, you can start to prepare. It's never too early. First, assess your diet, exercise, weight, and behavior. Next, knit some special heirloom pieces. With the three projects in this chapter, I hope to inspire you to start your own hope chest. Whether you're trying to conceive or pursuing adoption, this is a time to dream.

As you knit these special projects, picture holding your new baby and all the promise of the future that he or she holds. As I knitted each pinwheel square, I made a little wish for good health and a happy future. Now as I drape the blanket over the bed and watch my two beautiful, healthy children, I know that my wishes were heard.

TAKE-ME-HOME SWADDLE BLANKET

Swaddling is an ancient method of soothing a newborn by wrapping her snugly in a blanket. A baby with her arms tucked in close and snug in a wrapped blanket will drift off to sleep easier. Some say swaddling reminds a baby of her mother's womb. This blanket is made using a simple stitch pattern. Start it early. Knit a few inches each night, and in nine months, this blanket will be ready for the hospital bag. Knit in machine-washable wool, it is an easy-care choice for new parents scrambling to find enough time in the day to do all the household chores.

SKILL LEVEL
Easy

FINISHED MEASUREMENTS
38" (96.5cm) square

YARN
7 balls each of Dale of Norway Baby Ull, 100% machine-washable merino wool, 1¾ oz (50g), 180 yd (165m) in #6415 Turquoise (A) and #3507 Peach (B), (**1**) super fine

NEEDLES AND NOTIONS
- US size 10 (6mm) circular knitting needle, long enough to accommodate stitches, or size needed to obtain gauge
- US size I-9 (5.5mm) crochet hook
- Yarn needle

GAUGE
22 stitches and 32 rows = 4" (10cm) in linen stitch holding 1 strand each of A and B together.

Adjust needle size as necessary to obtain correct gauge.

NOTES
1. The Take-Me-Home Swaddle Blanket is knit back and forth in rows on a circular needle to accommodate the large number of stitches.
2. This stitch pattern requires an odd number of stitches. When testing your gauge, cast on 23 stitches and work in linen stitch.
3. The blanket is worked with 1 strand of each color held together throughout.

SWADDLE BLANKET
With 1 strand each of A and B held together, cast on 211 stitches.

Swaddling

HERE IS A QUICK SWADDLING
PRIMER. Lay the blanket flat.
Fold down the top corner. Lay
the baby down with her head
on the folded corner. Holding
her arms close to her body,
bring the right corner of the
blanket over and tuck it under
the baby. Fold the lower corner
up, over the legs, and then
fold the left corner around
and tuck under the baby.

LINEN STITCH

Row 1 (Right Side) K1, *with yarn
held in front, slip 1 stitch purlwise,
k1; repeat from * across.

Row 2 K1, p1, *with yarn held in
back, slip 1 stitch purlwise, p1;
repeat from * to last stitch, k1.

Repeat rows 1 and 2 until the
Blanket measures 38" (96.5cm)
from the beginning. Bind off.

EDGING

With 1 strand each of A and B held
together, join yarns in 1 corner,
single crochet evenly around edges
of Blanket; work 3 single crochet in
each corner. Slip stitch to first
single crochet to join. Fasten off.
Weave in ends. Lightly block.

Let's Make a Baby

THIS IS THE FUN PART. But before you try to conceive, you should take a few important steps.

1. Stop smoking, drinking, and using any other kind of drug. These habits are not healthy for you and can cause severe birth defects in your baby.

2. Adjust your diet. This is a perfect time to start eating healthy. Talk to your health care practitioner to help you develop and maintain a healthy diet.

3. Start taking a daily prenatal multivitamin that contains at least 400 milligrams of folic acid. Folic acid helps prevent certain birth defects.

4. Exercise daily. Strive for at least 30 minutes a day. You can just change a few habits to achieve this goal. For example, skip the elevators and escalators; park the car one block farther from your destination; walk the dog instead of putting her out in the backyard.

WHAT IF I'M ADOPTING A BABY? This process can be frustrating and confusing but definitely is worth the effort. The adoption route requires a few other steps:

1. Find an adoption agency in your area. Do your homework and research the company.

2. Look for adoptive parent networks and groups in your area. They are great places to ask for adopting agency recommendations.

3. Complete applications and paperwork.

4. Prepare to wait. This step is difficult. Waiting periods can range from 6 months to 5 years. Just remember, you're waiting for a precious gift, and in the end it's worth it! Think of all the knitting you'll get done!

Good luck!

KNITTED PINWHEEL QUILT

I love antique quilts. As a knitter, I wanted to create a knitted pinwheel quilt. After knitting my quilt, I looked through my linen closet for a good backing material and I found a favorite tablecloth that had one too many tea stains on it. I cut the tablecloth to fit the quilt. This is a great way to pass on a favorite linen that may be worse for wear. Scavenge your linen closet for a perfect match. The personal touch will make this hand-me-down into a treasured heirloom.

SKILL LEVEL

Intermediate

FINISHED MEASUREMENTS

20" (51cm) square

YARN

5 skeins of Blue Sky Alpacas Sport Weight, 100% baby alpaca, 1¾ oz (50g), 110 yd (100m) in #500 Natural White (A), **3** light

2 skeins each in #514 Pale Aqua (B), #515 Pistachio (C), #517 Lemondrop (D), #513 Peach (E), #516 Petal Pink (F)

NEEDLES AND NOTIONS

- US size 4 (3.5mm) knitting needles, or size needed to obtain gauge
- Bobbins
- Yarn needle
- Cotton quilt batting
- 22" (56cm) square of fabric for backing
- Straight pins
- Scissors

GAUGE

22 stitches and 30 rows = 4" (10cm) in stockinette stitch.

Adjust needle size as necessary to obtain correct gauge.

NOTES

1. The Pinwheel Squares are worked in intarsia, using a different ball of yarn for each color change. Wind bobbins for each color.
2. Pick up the new color from under the old color to twist the yarns and prevent holes.
3. The A color will be the main color in each square, with the contrasting color changing. Make 5 using A and B, 5 using A and C, 5 using A and D, 4 using A and E, and 5 using A and F. The center square will be a solid square using F.

4. The Squares are sewn together following the assembly diagram to make the quilt top.
5. A square of cotton batting is sandwiched between the knitted quilt top and backing fabric. All three layers are sewn together to make the quilt.

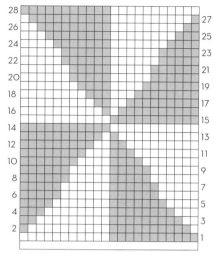

PINWHEEL CHART

28
26
24
22
20
18
16
14
12
10
8
6
4
2

27
25
23
21
19
17
15
13
11
9
7
5
3
1

22 Stitches

☐ = With A, k on right side,
p on wrong side

▨ = With B, C, D, E, or F,
k on right side,
p on wrong side

PINWHEEL SQUARES

Make 25 total: Make 5 with A and B, 5 with A and C, 5 with A and D, 4 with A and E, and 5 with A and F. The center square will be a solid square using F.

With A, cast on 22 stitches.

Row 1 K11 with contrasting color, k11 with A.

Row 2 P1 with contrasting color, p10 with A, p10 with contrasting color, p1 with A.

Row 3 K2 with A, k9 with contrasting color, k9 with A, k2 with contrasting color.

Row 4 P3 with contrasting color, p8 with A, p8 with contrasting color, p3 with A.

Row 5 K4 with A, k7 with contrasting color, k7 with A, k4 with contrasting color.

Row 6 P5 with A, p6 with contrasting color, p6 with A, p5 with contrasting color.

Row 7 K5 with A, k6 with contrasting color, k6 with A, k5 with contrasting color.

Row 8 P6 with contrasting color, p5 with A, p5 with contrasting color, p6 with A.

Row 9 K6 with A, k5 with contrasting color, k5 with A, k6 with contrasting color.

Row 10 P7 with contrasting color, p4 with A, p4 with contrasting color, p7 with A.

Row 11 K8 with A, k3 with contrasting color, k3 with A, k8 with contrasting color.

Row 12 P9 with contrasting color, p2 with A, p2 with contrasting color, p9 with A.

Row 13 K10 with A, k1 with contrasting color, k1 with A, k10 with contrasting color.

Row 14 P11 with A, p11 with contrasting color.

Row 15 K11 with contrasting color, k11 with A.

Row 16 P10 with A, p1 with contrasting color, p1 with A, p10 with contrasting color.

Row 17 K9 with contrasting color, k2 with A, k2 with contrasting color, k9 with A.

Row 18 P8 with A, p3 with contrasting color, p3 with A, p8 with contrasting color.

Row 19 K7 with contrasting color, k4 with A, k4 with contrasting color, k7 with A.

Row 20 P6 with A, p5 with contrasting color, p5 with A, p6 with contrasting color.

Row 21 K6 with contrasting color, k5 with A, k5 with contrasting color, k6 with A.

Row 22 P5 with A, p6 with contrasting color, p6 with A, p5 with contrasting color.

Row 23 K5 with contrasting color, k6 with A, k6 with contrasting color, k5 with A.

Row 24 P4 with A, p7 with contrasting color, p7 with A, p4 with contrasting color.

Row 25 K3 with contrasting color, k8 with A, k8 with contrasting color, k3 with A.

Row 26 P2 with A, p9 with contrasting color, p9 with A, p2 with contrasting color.

Row 27 K1 with contrasting color, k10 with A, k10 with contrasting color, k1 with A.

Row 28 P11 with contrasting color, p11 with A.

Bind off.

SOLID CENTER SQUARE

With F, cast on 22 stitches. Work in stockinette stitch for 28 rows. Bind off.

FINISHING

Using the assembly diagram, sew the squares together.

With yarn needle and A, embroider the baby's initials in the center square. Weave in ends. Lightly block.

Cut the cotton batting to ½" (1.5cm) larger than the quilt top. Arrange the cotton batting centered on the wrong side of the quilt top and pin. With right sides together, arrange the quilt top centered on the backing fabric and sew together along 3 edges, catching cotton batting in the edges securely. Clip corners of backing fabric and batting with fabric scissors. Turn piece right side out. Fold remaining open edge to wrong side, and whipstitch the side closed.

ASSEMBLY DIAGRAM

CHRISTENING GOWN

How does an heirloom become an heirloom? Who starts family traditions? Now that you're starting your family, why not also start some family traditions? This gown is a perfect opportunity. The skirt is knit in an easy lace pattern that will dare the novice knitter but not bore the experienced knitter. Knit this gown for your first or fifth child, and it will be treasured for generations to come. Share the gown with others. Lend it to nieces, nephews, and other loved ones. And let everyone leave their mark by signing the child's name to the ribbon. That's how traditions are created.

SKILL LEVEL
Intermediate

SIZES
0–6 months (12–24 months)

FINISHED MEASUREMENTS
Chest: 18 (22½)" (45.5 [57]cm)

Length: 36½ (40)" (92.5 [101.5]cm)

YARN
3 skeins of Jade Sapphire Silk/Cashmere 2-ply, 55% silk, 45% cashmere, 2 oz (55g), 400 yd (366m) in #000 Ivory, super fine

NEEDLES AND NOTIONS
- US size 1 (2.25mm) circular knitting needle, 24" (60cm) long, or size needed to obtain gauge
- US size 4 (3.5mm) circular knitting needle, 24" (60cm) long, or size needed to obtain gauge
- US size 1 (2.25mm) double-pointed knitting needles
- US size 4 (3.5mm) double-pointed knitting needles
- Stitch markers
- Stitch holders
- Yarn needle
- 2 yd (2m) cream double-faced satin ribbon, ¼" (6mm) wide

GAUGE
28 stitches and 36 rows = 4" (10cm) in blocked Lace Pattern using the larger needle

32 stitches and 40 rows = 4" (10cm) in stockinette stitch using the smaller needle

Adjust needle size as necessary to obtain correct gauge.

NOTES
1. The Gown is designed to fit a wide range of sizes. With the

LACE PATTERN 1

5 STITCHES

LACE PATTERN 2

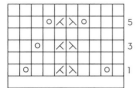

10 STITCHES

STITCH KEY

☐ = K on right side,
p on wrong side

╱ = K2tog on right side,
p2tog on wrong side

╲ = SSK on right side, p2tog
through back loops on
wrong side

⅄ = Slip 1 stitch, k2tog,
pass slipped stitch over

○ = Yarn over (yo)

use of a lovely ribbon and a well-placed eyelet row, the Gown can be cinched to the baby's chest measurements.

2. The lace patterns can be easily read row-by-row in the following text or by following the charts.

3. Remember to block your lace gauge swatch before measuring your gauge because the lace will "grow" in both length and width after blocking.

4. The Gown is knit from the bottom up in the round until the armhole, at which point the front and back of the bodice are worked separately, back and forth in rows.

5. The Sleeves are worked in the round and sewn to the finished bodice.

LACE PATTERN 1 (WORKED OVER 5 STITCHES)

Round 1 K1, yo, slip 1, k2tog, psso, yo, k1.

Round 2 Knit.

Repeat rounds 1 and 2 for Lace Pattern 1.

LACE PATTERN 2 (WORKED OVER 10 STITCHES)

Round 1 K1, yo, k2, ssk, k2tog, k2, yo, k1.

Round 2 and Every Even Row Knit.

Round 3 K2, yo, k1, ssk, k2tog, k1, yo, k2.

Round 5 K3, yo, ssk, k2tog, yo, k3.

Repeat rounds 1–6 for Lace Pattern 2.

SKIRT

With larger circular needle, cast on 180 (210) stitches. Join to work in the round, being careful not to twist the stitches; place a marker for the beginning of the round.

Purl 1 round.
Knit 1 round.
Purl 1 round.

Round 1 *Beginning with round 1, work 5 stitches of Lace Pattern 1, work 10 stitches of Lace Pattern 2; repeat from * around.

Continue to repeat the lace patterns until the skirt measures 29 (30)" (73 [76]cm) from beginning, ending with round 6 of lace pattern 2.

EYELET WAIST

Round 1 Purl.
Round 2 Knit.
Round 3 Purl.
Round 4 (Eyelet Round) * K2 (3), yo, k2tog; repeat from * around.
Round 5 Knit.
Round 6 Purl.
Round 7 *K3 (5), k2tog; repeat from * around—144 (180) stitches.
Round 8 Purl.

BODICE

Change to smaller circular needle, and work in stockinette stitch until the Bodice measures 3 (4)" (7.5 [10]cm), ending 4 stitches before beginning marker.

Divide for Front and Back

Note Bodice is divided at the armholes, and the Front and Back will be worked separately back and forth in rows.

Shape Armhole

Bind off 8 stitches, k64 (82) and slip stitches to a stitch holder for Front, bind off 8 stitches, k64 (82) stitches for Back.

BODICE BACK

Row 1 (Wrong Side) Purl—64 (82) stitches.
Row 2 K2, ssk, knit to last 4 stitches, k2tog, k2.

Repeat last 2 rows 3 more times—56 (74) stitches.

Continue to work in stockinette stitch until Bodice Back measures 4 (5)" (10 [12.5]cm), ending with a wrong-side row.

Divide for Button Band

Left Back

Next Row K28 (37) stitches, slip stitches to a stitch holder for the Right Back, join a second ball of yarn, and knit the remaining 28 (37) stitches for the Left Back.

Next Row (Wrong Side) Purl to last 3 stitches, k3.
Next Row Knit.

Repeat last 2 rows until the Left Back measures 7½ (9)" (19 [23]cm), ending with a right-side row.

Shape Shoulder and Neck

Next Row (Wrong Side) Bind off 20 (27) stitches, place remaining 8 (10) stitches on a stitch holder for the neck.

Right Back

With wrong side facing, slip stitches from the stitch holder to the needle.

Next Row (Wrong Side) K3, p25 (34) stitches.
Next Row Knit.

Repeat last 2 rows until the Right Back measures 7½ (9)" (19 [23]cm), ending with a wrong-side row.

Shape Shoulder and Neck

Next Row (Right Side) Bind off 20 (27) stitches, place remaining 8 (10) stitches on a stitch holder for the neck.

BODICE FRONT

With wrong side facing, slip stitches from the Front stitch holder to the needle.

Row 1 P64 (82) stitches.
Row 2 K2, ssk, knit to last 4 stitches, k2tog, k2.

Repeat last 2 rows 3 more times—56 (74) stitches.

Continue in stockinette stitch until the Bodice Front measures 6 (7½)" (15 [19]cm), ending with a wrong-side row.

Shape Neck

Next Row (Right Side) K21 (28) stitches and slip to a stitch holder for Left Shoulder, join a second ball of yarn and knit the center 14 (18) stitches for neck, slip to a stitch holder for neck, knit remaining 21 (28) stitches for Right Shoulder.

Right Shoulder

Next Row P21 (28) stitches.
Next Row K1, ssk, knit to end—20 (27) stitches.

Continue in stockinette stitch until the Front measures the same length as the Back to the shoulders. Bind off 20 (27) stitches.

Left Shoulder

With wrong side facing, slip stitches from the Left Shoulder stitch holder and purl 21 (28) stitches.

Next Row Knit to last 3 stitches, k2tog, k1—20 (27) stitches.

Continue in stockinette stitch until the Front measures the same length as the Back to the shoulders. Bind off 20 (27) stitches.

SLEEVES

Using larger double-pointed needles, cast on 75 (90) stitches and divide evenly among needles. Join to work in the round, being careful not to twist the stitches; place a marker for the beginning of the round.

Purl 1 round.
Knit 1 round.
Purl 1 round.

Round 1 *Work 5 stitches of Lace Pattern 1, work 10 stitches of Lace Pattern 2; repeat from * around.

Continue to work lace patterns through round 5.

Purl 1 round.
Next Round *K1, k2tog, yo; repeat from * around.
Knit 1 round.
Purl 1 round.

Change to smaller double-pointed needles and work in stockinette stitch until sleeve measures 6 (7½)" (15 [19]cm) from the beginning.

Shape Armhole

Note The Sleeve is divided at the armholes and will be worked back and forth in rows.

Row 1 Bind off 4 stitches, knit to end.

Row 2 Bind off 4 stitches, purl to end.

Next Row K1, ssk, knit to last 3 stitches, k2tog, k1.

Next Row Purl.

Repeat the last 2 rows 3 more times—59 (74) stitches.

Work in stockinette stitch until the Sleeve measures 7 (8½)" (18 [21.5]cm) from the beginning. Bind off.

FINISHING

Sew shoulders.

Neck band

Note Neck Band is worked back and forth in rows. Double-pointed knitting needles are used for ease in working around the Neck Band.

With right side facing and the smaller double-pointed knitting needles, join yarn and knit the 8 (10) stitches of the back Left Shoulder stitch holder, pick up and knit 7 (9) stitches from front left neck edge, knit the 14 (18) stitches from the front neck stitch holder, pick up and knit 7 (9) stitches from front right neck edge, knit remaining 8 (10) stitches from the back Right Shoulder holder—44 (56) stitches. Do not join; divide stitches evenly among needles.

Knit 1 row.

Buttonhole Row K2, yo, k2tog, knit to last 4 stitches, k2tog, yo, k2.

Knit 2 rows. Bind off loosely.

Weave in ends. Block lace on Sleeves and skirt to desired finished measurements. Sew Sleeves into the armholes.

Cut two 12" (30.5cm) lengths of cream ribbon and thread one length through the eyelets around each wrist.

Cut one length of cream ribbon 9" (23cm), and thread through the eyelets at the back neck to close.

Cut one length of cream ribbon 36" (91.5cm), and, beginning at the center Front, thread through the eyelets at the Waist.

It's Official

CONGRATULATIONS, YOU'RE EXPECTING! Over the next nine months, you may simultaneously feel excited, scared, overjoyed, overwhelmed, thrilled, and nauseated. Take all this in stride. Ask for help when you need it from your partner, children, doctors, and friends.

As an expectant knitter, the two most important issues at hand are your prenatal care and what to knit for the next nine months.

You have a lot of prenatal care options. When should you schedule your first appointment? Your doctor will first want to confirm your pregnancy with either a urinalysis or blood test. Once it's official that you are pregnant, your doctor will most likely schedule your first prenatal appointment between your eighth and tenth weeks of pregnancy.

You can expect a lot of activity at your first doctor's appointment. There will be a battery of tests and exams, including a pelvic exam, urine and blood tests, a physical exam of your uterus and your breasts, and a check of your blood pressure and weight. Also, the doctor will ask a series of questions ranging from family

history and medical history to the date of your last period.

You may be barraged with questions during this first appointment, but remember to ask questions, too. No question is stupid, especially during pregnancy. Your body is doing amazing and sometimes weird things. It is okay to mention when something seems off. Since it's easy to get overwhelmed, make a list of questions before each appointment. For your first appointment, here are a few suggestions:

1. Who do I call with questions between appointments?
2. What do you consider an emergency?
3. What do I do if I experience cramping or bleeding?
4. Do you have any diet suggestions?
5. Should I start taking vitamins?
6. When is my next appointment?

This chapter has many projects that even a beginner can knit. Explore the chapter, and find patterns to knit that will help you prepare for your new baby. Fill the wardrobe with easy-to knit sweaters, dresses, and pants. Hone your skills by knitting another intarsia project with the knitted blocks. Whichever project you choose, listen to the rhythm of your needles and relax—you have nine months to go. You're in for the ride of your life!

First Trimester

Week 1: Start taking your vitamins.

Week 2: Remember to eat a well-balanced diet.

Week 3: Early pregnancy indicators are mood swings, fatigue, and an uncontrollable urge to knit baby socks.

Week 4: Call in the vice squad. These early weeks are important for your baby's growth, so quit those bad habits.

Week 5: Visit your local yarn shop and select some soft, luxurious yarns for baby and you. The yarn shop owner is often the first to know.

Week 6: Remember to exercise. Pregnancy is not the time to stop your fitness routine. Just don't overdo it!

Week 7: Feeling a bit queasy? Try nibbling on crackers and sipping some ginger tea. Both will help soothe an unsteady stomach.

Week 8: Call and schedule your first doctor's appointment in the next two weeks.

Week 9: Feeling extra moody? Make yourself a nice cup of tea and curl up with your favorite ball of cashmere and a set of needles. Some indulgent knitting time is just what the doctor ordered.

Week 10: Dive into *The Expectant Knitter* and start knitting.

Week 11: Pregnancy craving? Pickles, ice cream, and Lorna's Laces Sportweight Happy Valley yarn? Just blame it on hormones.

Week 12: Pop! That's your bump beginning to show.

Week 13: Time to start knitting your baby's first sweater.

EASY RAGLAN SWEATER

An easy knitted sweater is a perfect place to start knitting your new baby's wardrobe. Knit from the top down in a cashmere-blend machine-washable yarn, it will quickly become your favorite sweater. And best of all, a wriggly baby can wear this sweater with the buttons facing front or back.

SKILL LEVEL
Easy

SIZES
0–6 months (12 months, 18 months, 24 months)

FINISHED MEASUREMENTS
Chest: 20 (21½, 23, 26)" (51 [54.5, 58.5, 66]cm) closed with a 4 (4, 4½, 4½)" (10 [10, 11.5, 11.5]cm) Front overlap

Length: 9 (10, 11½, 12)" (23 [25.5, 29, 30.5]cm)

YARN
3 (4, 5, 6) balls of Debbie Bliss Cashmerino Aran, 55% merino wool, 33% microfiber, 12% cashmere, 1¾ oz (50g), 98 yd (92m) in #502 Jade, (4) medium

NEEDLES AND NOTIONS
- US size 8 (5mm) circular needle, long enough to accommodate stitches, or size needed to obtain gauge
- US size 8 (5mm) double-pointed knitting needles
- US size E-4 (3.5mm) crochet hook
- Stitch markers
- Yarn needle
- 2 buttons, ½" (12mm) diameter

GAUGE
16 stitches and 28 rows = 4" (10cm) in stockinette stitch.

Adjust needle size as necessary to obtain correct gauge.

NOTES
1. The Easy Raglan Sweater is worked in 1 piece back and forth in rows from the neck down.
2. A circular needle is used to accommodate the large number of stitches.
3. The Sleeves are worked in the round on double-pointed knitting needles.
4. The neck and front edges have a 4-stitch seed stitch border.

ABBREVIATIONS
K1f&b: This is an easy increase stitch. Knit into the next stitch, but before removing it from the left-hand needle, knit again into the back loop of the same stitch. Remove the stitch from the left-hand needle—1 stitch increased.

YOU MAY BE KNITTING for two, but eating for two can be a recipe for disaster. Yes, you need extra calories from nutrient-rich foods to help your baby grow, but you really only need to consume an additional 100 to 300 calories to meet the needs of your growing baby.

Over the next several months, those extra calories will turn into approximately 30 pounds of:

7.5 pounds	baby
1.5 pounds	placenta
2 pounds	amniotic fluid
2 pounds	uterine enlargement
2 pounds	breast enlargement
4 pounds	blood volume
4 pounds	fluids in maternal tissue
7 pounds	fat stores

A well-balanced diet is the best strategy for appropriate weight gain and later successful loss of the baby fat. As with the morning sickness, a food diary can help guide your diet.

At the end of this trimester, your belly will definitely be showing. If you've had children before, this may happen earlier. The beautiful Shawl Sweater on page 117 is the perfect project to start and enjoy as your belly grows. The flattering shape and drape will also be a great option after the baby is born and the belly begins to disappear.

SEED STITCH

Row 1 *K1, p1; repeat from *.

Row 2 Knit the purl stitches and purl the knit stitches as they appear.

Repeat row 2 for seed stitch.

SWEATER

Starting at the neck, cast on 46 (48, 52, 54) stitches.

Work in seed stitch for 1" (2.5cm), ending with a wrong-side row.

Next Row (Right Side) K1, p1, k1, k1f&b, place marker, k1f&b, k3 (3, 4, 4), k1f&b, place marker, k1f&b, k14 (15, 16, 17), k1f&b, place marker, k1f&b, k3 (3, 4, 4), k1f&b, place marker, k1f&b, k10 (11, 12, 13), k1f&b, k1, p1, k1, p1—55 (57, 61, 63) stitches.

Row 1 (Wrong Side) Work in seed stitch for 4 stitches, purl to last 4 stitches, work in seed stitch for 4 stitches.

Row 2 (Right Side) Work in seed stitch for 4 stitches, *knit to 1 stitch before marker, k1f&b, slip marker, k1f&b; repeat from * 3 more times, knit to last 5 stitches, k1f&b, work in seed stitch for 4 stitches.

Repeat rows 1 and 2 for a total of 12 (13, 14, 15) times, ending with a wrong-side row—154 (165, 178, 189) stitches. The 16 (17, 18, 19) stitches to first marker are for the left front; the 29 (31, 34, 36) stitches to second marker are for the left sleeve; the 40 (43, 46, 49) stitches to third marker are for the back; the 29 (31, 34, 36) stitches to fourth marker are for the right sleeve, the last 40 (43, 46, 49) stitches are for the right front.

Divide for Sleeves

With right side facing, work in seed stitch for 4 stitches, knit to second marker and slip the last 29 (31, 34, 36) stitches just worked to stitch holder for left sleeve, knit to fourth marker and slip the last 29 (31, 34, 36) stitches just worked to stitch holder for right sleeve, knit to last 4 stitches, work in seed stitch for 4 stitches.

BODY

Next Row (Wrong Side) Work in seed stitch for 4 stitches, purl to first marker, remove marker, cast on 4 stitches, remove second marker, purl to third marker, remove marker, cast on 4 stitches, remove fourth marker, purl to last 4 stitches, work in seed stitch for 4 stitches—96 (103, 110, 117) stitches.

Continue working first and last 4 stitches of every row in seed stitch while working in stockinette stitch for all other stitches until the sweater measures 9 (10, 11½, 12)" (23 [25.5, 29, 30.5]cm) inches from the cast-on edge.

Work 1" (2.5cm) in seed stitch for border.

Bind off in pattern.

SLEEVES

With right side facing and double-pointed knitting needles, join yarn at center of 4-stitch cast-on at underarm and pick up 2 stitches along the cast-on edge, k29 (31, 34, 36) stitches from the stitch holder, pick up 2 stitches along the cast-on edge, place marker for beginning of round—33 (35, 38, 40) stitches. Divide stitches evenly among needles.

Knit 3 (4, 1, 5) rounds.

*Decrease Round K1, ssk, knit to last 3 stitches, k2tog, k1.

Work 5 (6, 7, 8) rounds.

Repeat from * 2 (2, 3, 3) more times—27 (29, 30, 32) stitches. Sleeve measures 4¾ (5¾, 6, 6½)" (12 [14.5, 15, 16.5]cm) from the pick-up row.

Work in seed stitch for 1" (2.5cm) for border. Bind off.

FINISHING

Weave in ends. Lightly block.

Using crochet hook, join yarn at outer corner of right front neck. Chain 3 stitches, slip stitch in same space for buttonhole loop. Chain second buttonhole loop at right front underarm.

Sew buttons opposite buttonhole loops on right front.

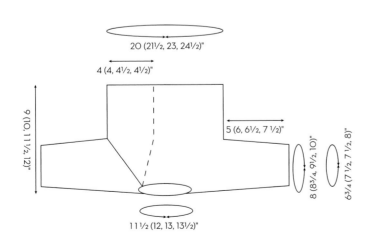

20 (21½, 23, 24½)"

4 (4, 4½, 4½)"

9 (10, 11½, 12)"

5 (6, 6½, 7½)"

8 (8¾, 9½, 10)"

6¾ (7½, 7½, 8)"

11½ (12, 13, 13½)"

HER FIRST PARTY DRESS

This silky-soft, cabled yoke dress will please any little girl, any day of the week. With yoke collar and generous sizing, this dress is designed to grow along with her. You can safely knit this knowing that your princess will wear it over and over again—it will never go out of style. Refresh the ribbon, and pass the dress on to another lucky little girl when the first has outgrown it.

SKILL LEVEL
Intermediate

SIZES
0-9 months (12-18 months, 24-36 months)

FINISHED MEASUREMENTS
Chest: 24½ (28, 34½)" (62 [71, 87.5]cm)

Length: 13 (16, 19)" (33 [40.5, 48]cm)

YARN
3 (4, 5) skeins of Blue Sky Alpacas Alpaca Silk, 50% baby alpaca, 50% silk, 1¾ oz (50g), 146 yd (133m) in #114 Wisteria, **1** super fine

NEEDLES AND NOTIONS
- US size 3 (3.25mm) circular knitting needle, long enough to accommodate stitches, or size needed to obtain gauge
- Cable needle
- Yarn needle
- 1 yd (1m) red double-faced satin ribbon, ¼" (6mm) wide

- 1 matching pearl button, ½" (12mm) diameter

GAUGE
28 stitches and 32 rows = 4" (10cm) in stockinette stitch.

Adjust needle size as necessary to obtain correct gauge.

NOTES
1. The fit is very generous. The same dress is worn by both our eight-month-old and two-and-a-half-year-old models. The satin ribbon is used to cinch the chest to a closer desired fit.
2. The Dress is knit back and forth in rows on a circular needle to accommodate the large number of stitches.
3. The Dress is knit from the neck down.

ABBREVIATIONS
C2F: Slip next stitch to cable needle and hold in front. Knit the next stitch from the left-hand needle. Return the stitch from the cable needle to the left-hand needle and knit it.

C4F: Slip next 2 stitches to a cable needle and hold in front. Knit the next 2 stitches from the left-hand needle. Knit the stitches from the cable needle.

C6F: Slip next 3 stitches to cable needle and hold in front. Knit the next 3 stitches from the left-hand needle. Knit the stitches from the cable needle.

K1f&b: This is an easy increase stitch. Knit into the next stitch, but before removing the old stitch from the left-hand needle, knit again into the back loop of the same stitch. Remove the old stitch from the left-hand needle—1 stitch increased.

P1f&b: This is an easy increase stitch. Purl into the next stitch, but before removing the old stitch from the left-hand needle, purl again into the back loop of the same stitch. Remove the old stitch from the left-hand needle—1 stitch increased.

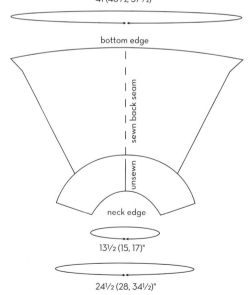

41 (46½, 57½)"

bottom edge

sewn back seam

unsewn

neck edge

13½ (15, 17)"

24½ (28, 34½)"

DRESS

Starting at the neck edge, cast on 94 (103, 121) stitches.

Row 1 (Wrong Side) Purl across.
Row 2 (Right Side) P1, *k2, p1; repeat from * across.
Row 3 K1, *p2, k1; repeat from * across.
Row 4 P1, * C2F, p1; repeat from * across.
Row 5 K1, *p2, k1; repeat from * across.
Row 6 P1f&b, *k2, p1f&b; repeat from * across—126 (138, 162) stitches.
Row 7 K2, *p2, k2; repeat from * across.
Row 8 P2, *C2F, p2; repeat from * across.
Row 9 K2, *(p1f&b) twice, k2; repeat from * across—188 (206, 242) stitches.
Row 10 P2, *k4, p2; repeat from * across.
Row 11 K2, *p4, k2; repeat from * across.
Row 12 P2, *C4F, p2; repeat from * across.
Row 13 K2, *p4, k2; repeat from * across.
Row 14 P2, *k4, p2; repeat from * across.
Row 15 K1, k1f&b, *p4, k1, k1f&b; repeat from * across—220 (241, 283) stitches.
Row 16 P3, *C4F, p3; repeat from * across.
Row 17 K3, *p1f&b, p2, p1f&B, k3; repeat from * to the end of the row—282 (309, 363) stitches.

Row 18 P3, *k6, p3; repeat from * across.

Row 19 K3, *p6, k3; repeat from * across.

Row 20 P3, *C6F, p3; repeat from * across.

Row 21 Repeat row 19.

Row 22 Repeat row 18.

Row 23 Repeat row 19.

Row 24 Repeat row 18.

Repeat rows 19–24 0 (0, 1) more times.

Shape Sleeve Caps

Next Row (Wrong Side) K37 (43, 54), bind off 66 (68, 72) stitches, k76 (87, 111), bind off 66 (68, 72) stitches, k37 (43, 54).

Next Row P37 (43, 54), cast on 8 (11, 12) stitches, p76 (87, 110), cast on 8 (11, 12) stitches, p37 (43, 54)—166 (195, 242) stitches.

Eyelet Row P3 (3, 2), *yo, p2tog, p1; repeat from * across.

Purl 1 row.

Knit 1 row.

Continue to work in stockinette stitch until the Dress measures 9 (12, 14½)" (23 [30.5, 37]cm) from Eyelet Row.

Ruffle

Row 1 KO (O, 2), *k1f&b, k2; repeat from * across—228 (260, 322) stitches.

Work in stockinette stitch for 3 rows.

Row 5 K2 (O, 2), *k1f&b, k3; repeat from * across—285 (325, 402) stitches.

Work in stockinette stitch for 3 rows. Bind off.

FINISHING

Sew back seam closed, ending 3" (7.5cm) from neck edge.

Sew button at the back neck edge. Create an afterthought buttonhole by inserting thread into upper corner of back neck edge. Create a simple loop by holding thread and inserting yarn needle ½" (1.5cm) from neck edge. Knot the ends together to use as a button loop.

Block dress as desired. I suggest wet-blocking, which will soften the cable yoke.

Beginning and ending at the center of the front, thread ribbon length through the eyelets. Tie the ends into a bow.

Morning Sickness

DOES MORNING SICKNESS MEAN I'M HAVING A BOY OR A GIRL? One wives' tale says that morning sickness is an indicator that you're having a boy. Another says that it's definite you're carrying a girl. Either way, morning sickness can take the wind out of your sails.

Morning sickness is very common. Some reports indicate more than half of all pregnant women experience some symptoms. It can start as early as your sixth week and usually continues until your fourteenth to sixteenth week of pregnancy. Symptoms of morning sickness can range from occasional vomiting to all-day nausea. If vomiting is followed by cramping, bleeding, or a fever, call your health-care provider.

When I was pregnant with Cole, I was more nauseated than I had been with Nora. I found that I reacted to certain foods. Red meat was a major trigger. As a steak lover, this was very stressful. But I consider myself fortunate that my symptoms were very, very mild. I learned to avoid my trigger foods and look forward to the next trimester. Here are some tips to help you cope:

1. Talk about it. Tell your practitioner about your morning sickness symptoms and ask for support and suggestions.

2. Pop a cracker. Carry a ready supply of crackers so your stomach will never get empty.

3. Know the enemy: Certain foods may trigger stronger symptoms. Start a food diary and note how you react to different dishes. This will help to guide your eating habits.

4. Size matters. Try eating smaller, more frequent meals during the day. This strategy will help to prevent an empty stomach, which can trigger stronger symptoms.

5. Take your vitamins. Your prenatal vitamins will ensure that you obtain the necessary nutrients for you and your growing baby.

6. Knit in color. Brighten your day with a fun and easy project. The Easy Raglan Sweater on page 32 is a perfect distraction. Choose a warm color and relish in the soothing rhythm of the needles as you knit your first sweater for baby.

CABLED SWEATER VEST

Sometimes the best part of baby projects is the size. Pint-sized knits are fast, and this little vest is simply adorable. Try out your cabling skills with a simple center braided cable. Knit in cashmere-soft yet bulky yarn, this clever vest is sure to become your "go-to" knitted baby project. Sized from newborn to toddler, it is a perfect gift for any special boy or girl.

SKILL LEVEL
Intermediate

SIZES
0–3 months (6–9 months, 12 months, 18–24 months)

FINISHED MEASUREMENTS
Chest: 18 (21, 22, 25)" (45.5 [53.5, 56, 63.5]cm)

Length: 10½ (12, 13, 14)" (26.5 [30.5, 33, 35.5]cm)

YARN
2 (3, 3, 4) balls of Debbie Bliss Cashmerino Superchunky, 55% merino wool, 33% microfiber, 12% cashmere, 3½ oz (100g), 82 yd (75m) in #13 Bright White, (5) bulky

NEEDLES AND NOTIONS
- US size 10 (6mm) knitting needles
- US size 11 (8mm) knitting needles, or size needed to obtain gauge
- US size 10 (6mm) double-pointed knitting needles
- Cable needle
- Stitch holders
- Yarn needle

GAUGE
12 stitches and 16 rows = 4" (10cm) in stockinette stitch using larger needles

Adjust needle size as necessary to obtain correct gauge.

ABBREVIATIONS
C6F: Slip next 3 stitches to cable needle and hold in front. Knit the next 3 stitches from the left-hand needle. Knit the stitches from the cable needle.

C6B: Slip next 3 stitches to cable needle and hold in back. Knit the next 3 stitches from the left-hand needle. Knit the stitches from the cable needle.

BACK
With smaller needles, cast on 27 (31, 33, 37) stitches.

Row 1 (Wrong Side) P1, *k1, p1; repeat from * across.
Row 2 (Right Side) K1, *p1, k1; repeat from * across.

Repeat rows 1 and 2 until piece measures 1½ (1½, 2, 2)" (4 [4, 5, 5]cm) from the beginning, ending with a wrong-side row. Change to larger needles.

Schematic

4½ (5, 5½, 5½)"

1½"

FRONT AND BACK

4 (4½, 5, 5)"

6· (7½, 8, 9)"

9 (10½, 11, 12½)"

BRAIDED CABLE

8
7
6
5
4
3
2
1

9 STITCHES

STITCH KEY

☐ = K on right side, p on wrong side

• = P on right side, k on wrong side

 = Slip 3 stitches onto cable needle and hold in back, k3, k3 from cable needle

= Slip 3 stitches onto cable needle and hold in front, k3, k3 from cable needle

Begin Braided Cable Pattern

Note There are 6 (8, 9, 11) stitches on each side of the Braided Cable pattern. If you choose to use the chart, be sure to work those required 6 (8, 9, 11) stitches on either side of the Cable pattern.

Row 1 (Right Side) K6 (8, 9, 11) (these center 15 stitches are the Braided Cable pattern stitches) p3, k9, p3, k6 (8, 9, 11).

Row 2 P6 (8, 9, 11), k3, p9, k3, p6 (8, 9, 11).

Row 3 K6 (8, 9, 11), p3, C6F, k3, p3, k6 (8, 9, 11).

Row 4 P6 (8, 9, 11), k3, p9, k3, p6 (8, 9, 11).

Row 5 K6 (8, 9, 11), p3, k9, p3, k6 (8, 9, 11).

Row 6 P6 (8, 9, 11), k3, p9, k3, p6 (8, 9, 11).

Row 7 K6 (8, 9, 11), p3, k3, C6B, p3, k6 (8, 9, 11).

Row 8 P6 (8, 9, 11), k3, p9, k3, p6 (8, 9, 11).

Repeat rows 1–8 until the piece measures 6½ (7½, 8, 9)" (16.5 [19, 20.5, 23]cm) from the beginning, ending with a wrong-side row.

Shape Armhole

Bind off 2 stitches at the beginning of the next 2 rows.

Continue in established pattern until piece measures 10½ (12, 13, 14)" (26.5 [30.5, 33, 35.5]cm) from beginning, ending with a wrong-side row.

Shape Neck and Shoulders

Next Row (Right Side) Bind off 5 (6, 6, 8) stitches, join a new ball of yarn, and work center 13 (15, 17, 17) stitches in pattern and slip onto a stitch holder for back neck; knit to end.

Next Row Bind off 5 (6, 6, 8) stitches.

FRONT

Work same as for the Back until the piece measures 9 (10½, 11½, 12½)" (23 [26.5, 29, 32]cm) from the beginning, ending with a wrong-side row.

Shape Neck and Shoulders

Next Row (Right Side) K6 (7, 7, 9) stitches and slip to a stitch holder for Left Shoulder, join a new ball of yarn, and work center 11 (13, 15, 15) stitches in pattern and slip onto a stitch holder for front neck; knit to end.

Right Shoulder

Next Row (Wrong Side) Work in pattern to the last 2 stitches, k2tog—5 (6, 6, 8) stitches.

Continue in pattern until the piece measures the same length as the Back to the shoulders. Bind off 5 (6, 6, 8) stitches.

Left Shoulder

Next Row (Wrong Side) Slip stitches from stitch holder to needles and k2tog, work in pattern to end—5 (6, 6, 8) stitches.

Continue in pattern until the piece measures the same length as the Back to the shoulders. Bind off 5 (6, 6, 8) stitches.

FINISHING

Sew shoulder seams together.

Neck Edging

With right side facing and smaller double-pointed knitting needles, join yarn at Left Shoulder edge, pick up and knit 6 stitches, k11 (13, 15, 15) stitches from front neck stitch holder, pick up and knit 6 stitches from right side, k13 (15, 17, 17) stitches from Back holder—36 (40, 44, 44) stitches. Divide stitches evenly among needles. Join to work in the round, being careful not to twist the stitches; place a marker for the beginning of the round.

Rib

Round 1 (K1, p1) around.

Repeat round 1 for 4 rounds. Bind off loosely in pattern.

Armhole Edging

Sew side seams together.

With right side facing and smaller double-pointed knitting needles, join yarn at underarm, pick up and knit 32 (36, 40, 42) stitches around armhole. Divide stitches evenly among needles. Join to work in the round, being careful not to twist the stitches; place a marker for the beginning of the round.

Work in rib for 5 rounds.

Weave in ends. Lightly block.

CASHMERE ROMPER

"Soft as a baby's bottom, light as a feather" aptly describes this luxurious cashmere romper. Knit in 8-ply cashmere, this quick knit is worth every minute of your time. Simple shaping and bold colors will make it a favorite in every child's wardrobe.

SKILL LEVEL
Easy

SIZES
0–6 months (12 months, 18-24 months)

FINISHED MEASUREMENTS
Chest: 22 (26, 29)" (56 [66, 73.5]cm)

Length: 20 (22½, 24½)" (51 [57, 62]cm)

YARN
3 (4, 4) balls of Classic Elite Yarns Obsession, 100% cashmere, 1¾ oz (50g), 95 yd (87m) in #H60584 Aqua, (**5**) bulky

NEEDLES AND NOTIONS
- US size 11 (8mm) knitting needles, or size needed to obtain gauge
- US size I-9 (5.5mm) crochet hook
- Stitch holders
- Yarn needle
- 6 buttons, 1" (2.5cm) diameter

GAUGE
12 stitches and 16 rows = 4" (10cm) in stockinette stitch

Adjust needle size as necessary to obtain correct gauge.

NOTE
The Front and Back are worked the same.

BACK

First Leg
Cast on 15 (17, 19) stitches.

Work in stockinette stitch until the Leg measures 7 (9, 10)" (18 [23, 25.5]cm) from the beginning, ending with a wrong-side row. Slip stitches to a stitch holder.

Second Leg
Work as for the First Leg.

Join Legs to Body
Next Row (Right Side) K15 (17, 19) stitches from one First Leg stitch holder, cast on 3 (5, 5) stitches, knit 15 (17, 19) stitches from Second Leg stitch holder—33 (39, 43) stitches.

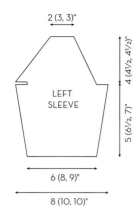

2 (3, 3)"

4 (4½, 4½)"

5 (6½, 7)"

LEFT
SLEEVE

6 (8, 9)"

8 (10, 10)"

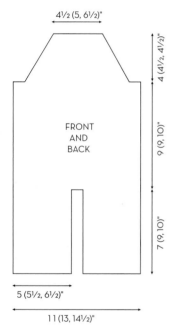

4½ (5, 6½)"

4 (4½, 4½)"

9 (9, 10)"

FRONT
AND
BACK

7 (9, 10)"

5 (5½, 6½)"

11 (13, 14½)"

Continue in stockinette stitch until the piece measures 16 (18, 20)" (40.5 [45.5, 51]cm) from the beginning, ending with a wrong-side row.

Shape Armhole

Bind off 3 stitches at the beginning of the next 2 rows—27 (33, 37) stitches.

Decrease Row (Right Side) K1, ssk, knit to last 3 stitches, k2tog, k1.

Purl 1 row.

Repeat last 2 rows 6 (8, 8) more times—13 (15, 19) stitches.

Bind off.

FRONT

Work as for the Back.

LEFT SLEEVE

Cast on 18 (24, 27) stitches.

Work in stockinette stitch for 5 (7, 7) rows.

Increase 1 stitch at each edge every 4 (6, 6) row 3 (3, 2) times—24 (30, 31) stitches.

Continue in stockinette stitch until the Sleeve measures 5 (6½,

7)" (12.5 [15, 18]cm) from the beginning, ending with the wrong side facing.

Shape Armhole

Bind off 2 stitches at the beginning of the next 2 rows.

Next Row (Right Side) Knit across, place marker, cast on 3 stitches—23 (29, 30) stitches. Next Row K3, slip marker, purl across.

Decrease Row K1, ssk, knit to 3 stitches before the marker, k2tog, k1, slip marker, knit to end.

Repeat the last 2 rows 7 (9, 9) more times—7 (9, 9) stitches.

Bind off.

RIGHT SLEEVE

Work as for the Left Sleeve to Armhole.

Shape Armhole

Bind off 2 stitches at the beginning of the next 2 rows.

Next Row (Right Side) Cast on 3 stitches, place marker, knit across—23 (29, 30) stitches.
Next Row Purl across to last 3 stitches, slip marker, k3.

Decrease Row K3, slip marker, k1, ssk, knit to last 3 stitches, k2tog, k1.

Repeat the last 2 rows 7 (9, 9) more times—7 (9, 9) stitches.

Bind off.

FINISHING
Sew Front and Back side seams. Sew raglan edges of Sleeves to the Back only, leaving the 3-stitch garter stitch border open on the Front. Sew on three buttons evenly spaced on each side in the 3-stitch garter stitch border.

Edging
With crochet hook, join yarn at neck edge and single crochet around the raglan opening, working chain 2, skip a space for button, along Front raglan edge opposite each button. Sew Sleeve seams.

Weave in ends. Lightly block.

MATINEE SWEATER

This dainty cardigan is for a little girl, who can wear it over her favorite dress to keep away the morning chill. Knit from the neck down, this light sweater requires minimal shaping and finishing. Change the look with a simple change of ribbon.

SKILL LEVEL
Easy

SIZES
0–9 months (9–18 months, 18–24 months)

FINISHED MEASUREMENTS
Chest: 25 (26, 29)" (63.5 [66, 73.5]cm)

Length: 9½ (11, 13)" (24 [28, 33]cm)

YARN
2 (3, 4) skeins of Blue Sky Alpacas Alpaca Silk, 50% baby alpaca, 50% silk, 1¾ oz (50g), 146 yd (133m) in #133 Blush, (**1**) super fine

NEEDLES AND NOTIONS
- US size 3 (3.25mm) circular knitting needle, long enough to accommodate stitches, or size needed to obtain gauge
- Yarn needle
- 1 (1½, 1½) yd (1 [1½, 1½]m) pale pink double-faced satin ribbon, ¼" (6mm) wide

GAUGE
24 stitches and 32 rows = 4" (10cm) in stockinette stitch.

Adjust needle size as necessary to obtain correct gauge.

NOTES
1. The sweater is worked in one piece back and forth in rows from the neck down.
2. A circular needle is used to accommodate the large number of stitches.

ABBREVIATIONS
K1f&b: This is an easy increase stitch. Knit into the next stitch, but before removing the old stitch from the left-hand needle, knit again into the back loop of the same stitch. Remove the old stitch from the left-hand needle— 1 stitch increased.

YOKE
Cast on 61 (65, 73) stitches.

Row 1 (Right Side) K1, *p1, k1; repeat from * across.

Row 2 P1, *k1, p1; repeat from * across.

Work the last 2 rows 1 (1, 2) times, then row 1 once.

Increase Row (Wrong Side)
Note The first stitch of this row is different for the different sizes. Only size 0–9 months works k1f&b; sizes 9–18 months and 18–24 months knit 1.

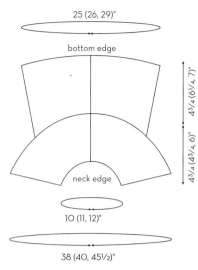

25 (26, 29)"

bottom edge

neck edge

4³/₄ (6¹/₄, 7)"

4³/₄ (4³/₄, 6)"

4³/₄ (4³/₄, 6)"

10 (11, 12)"

38 (40, 45¹/₂)"

K1f&b (k1, k1), *k3, k1f&b; repeat from * across—77 (81, 91) stitches. Knit 2 rows.

Row 1 (Right Side) K1, *p1, k1; repeat from * across. Work in rib for 4 (4, 6) more rows.

Increase Row K1, *k1f&b, k1; repeat from * across—115 (121, 136) stitches. Knit 2 rows.

Row 1 (Right Side) K1, *p1, k1; repeat from * across, end p0 (0, 1). Work in rib for 4 (4, 6) more rows.

Increase Row K1 (1, 0), *k1f&b, k1; repeat from * across—172 (181, 204) stitches. Knit 2 rows.

Row 1 (Right Side) K1, *p1, k1; repeat from * across, end p1 (0, 1). Work in rib for 4 (4, 6) more rows.

Increase Row K1 (1, 0), *k1f&b, k2; repeat from, * across—229 (241, 272) stitches. Knit 2 rows.

Row 1 (Right Side) K1, *p1, k1; repeat from * across, end p0 (0, 1). Work in rib for 4 (4, 6) more rows. Knit 1 row.

Shape Armhole

Next Row (Right Side) K33 (35, 39), bind off 48 (50, 58) stitches, k67 (71, 78), bind off 48 (50, 58) stitches, k33 (35, 39)—133 (141, 156) stitches.

BODY

Next Row K33 (35, 39), cast on 8 (8, 9) stitches, k67 (71, 78), cast on 8 (8, 9) stitches, k33 (35, 39)—149 (157, 174) stitches.

Eyelet Row K1 (1, 2), *yo, k2tog, k2; repeat from * across. Knit 1 row.

Continue in stockinette stitch until the sweater measures 5 (6, 7)" (12.5 [15, 18]cm) from the Eyelet row. Bind off.

FINISHING

Weave in ends. Lightly block. Beginning and ending at the center of the front, thread the ribbon length through the Eyelet Row.

GIRL'S SUMMER SUIT

What do you knit for a summer baby? Any little girl will love to receive this two-piece summer suit. Made with the softest cotton, this top and diaper cover set is so light and airy that even the hottest summer days will not wilt your summer flower.

SKILL LEVEL
Easy

SIZES
0–6 months (12 months, 18 months, 24 months)

FINISHED MEASUREMENTS
Chest: 15½ (16½, 18, 20)" (39.5 [42, 45.5, 51]cm)

Length: 8 (9, 9½, 10)" (20.5 [23, 24, 25.5]cm)

Diaper Cover Waist: 16 (18, 20, 22)" (40.5 [45.5, 51, 56]cm)

YARN
For Top
1 (1, 2, 2) skeins each of Blue Sky Alpacas Dyed Cotton, 100% organically grown cotton, 3½ oz (100g), 150 yd (137m) in #606 Shell (A) and #615 Tulip (B), 🧶 medium

For Diaper Cover
1 skein each of Blue Sky Alpacas Dyed Cotton, 100% organically grown cotton, 3½ oz (100g), 150 yd (137m) in #615 Tulip, 🧶 medium

NEEDLES AND NOTIONS
- US size 7 (4.5mm) knitting needles
- US size 8 (5mm) knitting needles, or size needed to obtain gauge
- US size H-8 (5mm) crochet hook
- Yarn needle
- 1 yd (1m) twill ribbon tape, ⅝" (1.5cm) wide
- 1 button, ½" (1.5cm) diameter

GAUGE
16 stitches and 24 rows = 4" (10cm) in stockinette stitch

Adjust needle size as necessary to obtain correct gauge.

NOTE
This summer top is closed in the back with a small button. The chest measurement is close to the body, but the skirt flares to accommodate a wide range of sizes.

TOP FRONT
With larger needles and A, cast on 40 (44, 48, 52) stitches.

Work in stockinette stitch until the piece measures 3½ (4, 4½, 5)" (9 [10, 11.5, 12]cm) from the beginning, ending with a wrong-side row.

Next Row (Right Side) *P2tog, p2; repeat from * across—30 (33, 36, 39) stitches.
Change to B and knit 1 row.

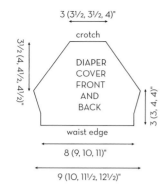

3 (3½, 3½, 4)"

crotch

DIAPER
COVER
FRONT
AND
BACK

3½ (4, 4½, 4½)"

3 (3, 4, 4)"

waist edge

8 (9, 10, 11)"

9 (10, 11½, 12½)"

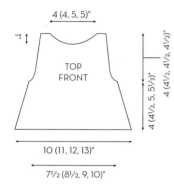

4 (4, 5, 5)"

TOP
FRONT

4 (4½, 5, 5½)"

4 (4½, 4½, 4½)"

10 (11, 12, 13)"

7½ (8½, 9, 10)"

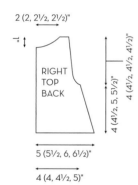

2 (2, 2½, 2½)"

RIGHT
TOP
BACK

4 (4½, 5, 5½)"

4 (4½, 4½, 4½)"

5 (5½, 6, 6½)"

4 (4, 4½, 5)"

Work in stockinette stitch for
2 rows.

Shape Armholes

Bind off 2 stitches at the
beginning of the next 2 rows—26
(29, 32, 35) stitches.

Next Row K1, k2tog, knit to last 3
stitches, ssk, k1—24 (27, 30, 33)
stitches.

Work in stockinette stitch until
the piece measures 7½ (8, 8½,
9)" (19 [20.5, 21.5, 23]cm from
the beginning, ending with a
wrong-side row.

Shape Shoulders

Next Row (Right Side) K7 (8, 8,
9) and slip these stitches to a
stitch holder for the left shoulder,
join a new ball of yarn, and bind
off 10 (11, 14, 15) stitches for the
neck, k7 (8, 8, 9) for right
shoulder.

Right Shoulder

Next Row P7 (8, 8, 9) stitches.
Next Row K1, ssk, k1 (2, 2, 3),
k2tog, k1—5 (6, 6, 7) stitches.
Purl 1 row.

Next Row K1, ssk, k2tog, k0 (1, 1,
2)—3 (4, 4, 5) stitches.
Purl 1 row.

For 0–6 Months Size Only
Bind off.

For All Other Sizes
Next Row Ssk, k2tog, k- (0, 0, 1)—
- (2, 2, 3) stitches.
Purl 1 row.

Bind off.

Left Shoulder

Next Row P7 (8, 8, 9) stitches.
Next Row K1, ssk, k1 (2, 2, 3),
k2tog, k1—5 (6, 6, 7) stitches.
Purl 1 row.

Next Row K1, ssk, k2tog, k0 (1, 1,
2)—3 (4, 4, 5) stitches.
Purl 1 row.

For 0–6 Months Size Only
Bind off.

For All Other Sizes
Next Row Ssk, k2tog, k- (0, 0, 1)—
- (2, 2, 3) stitches.
Purl 1 row.

Bind off.

RIGHT TOP BACK

With larger needles and A, cast
on 20 (22, 24, 26) stitches.

Work in stockinette stitch until
the piece measures 3½ (4, 4½,
5)" (9 [10, 11.5, 12]cm) from the
beginning, ending with a wrong-
side row.

Next Row (Right Side) *P2tog, p2; repeat from * across to last O (2, O, 2)—15 (17, 18, 20) stitches.

Change to B and knit 1 row.

Work in stockinette stitch for 2 rows.

Shape Armholes
At the beginning of the next right-side row, bind off 2 stitches—13 (15, 16, 18) stitches.

Purl 1 row.
Next Row K1, k2tog, knit to end—12 (14, 15, 17) stitches.

Work in stockinette stitch until the piece measures 7½ (8, 8½, 9)" (19 [20.5, 21.5, 23]cm) from beginning, ending with a right-side row.

Shape Neck
Next Row (Wrong Side) Bind off 5 (6, 7, 8) stitches, purl across—7 (8, 8, 9) stitches.
Next Row K1, ssk, k1 (2, 2, 3), k2tog, k1—5 (6, 6, 7) stitches.
Purl 1 row.

Next Row K1, ssk, k2tog, kO (1, 1, 2)—3 (4, 4, 5) stitches.
Purl 1 row.

For O–6 Month Size Only
Bind off.

For All Other Sizes
Next Row Ssk, k2tog, k- (O, O, 1)—- (2, 2, 3) stitches.

Purl 1 row.

Bind off.

LEFT TOP BACK
With larger needles and A, cast on 20 (22, 24, 26) stitches.

Work in stockinette stitch until the piece measures 3½ (4, 4½, 5)" (9 [10, 11.5, 12]cm) from the beginning, ending with a wrong-side row.

Next Row (Right Side) *P2tog, p2; repeat from * across to last O (2, O, 2)—15 (17, 18, 20) stitches.

Change to B and knit 1 row.

Work in stockinette stitch for 3 rows.

Shape Armholes
At the beginning of the next wrong-side row, bind off 2 stitches—13 (15, 16, 18) stitches.

Next Row K1, k2tog, knit to end—12 (14, 15, 17) stitches.

Work in stockinette stitch until the piece measures 7½ (8, 8½, 9)" (19 [20.5, 21.5, 23]cm) from the beginning, ending with a wrong-side row.

Shape Neck
Next Row (Right Side) Bind off 5 (6, 7, 8) stitches, knit across—7 (8, 8, 9) stitches.
Purl 1 row.

Next Row K1, ssk, k1 (2, 2, 3), k2tog, k1—5 (6, 6, 7) stitches. Purl 1 row.

Next Row K1, ssk, k2tog, k0 (1, 1, 2)—3 (4, 4, 5) stitches. Purl 1 row.

For 0–6 Month Size Only
Bind off.

For All Other Sizes
Next Row Ssk, k2tog, k- (0, 0, 1)—- (2, 2, 3) stitches.
Purl 1 row.

Bind off.

TOP FINISHING

Lightly steam-block the pieces. Sew the side seams and shoulder seams. Sew a button on the right back neck edge. Using a crochet hook, join yarn on the left back at the neck edge opposite the button and work a chain stitch loop for the button. Weave in the ends.

DIAPER COVER BACK

With smaller needles and B, cast on 32 (36, 40, 44) stitches.

Row 1 *K1, p1; repeat from * across.

Repeat row 1 for 2 more rows.

Eyelet Row K1, *k2tog, yo; repeat from * to last stitch, k1.

Repeat row 1 for 2 more rows.

Change to larger needles and garter stitch as follows:
Rows 1–5 Knit
Row 6 K1, k1f&b, knit to the last 2 stitches, k1f&b, k1.

Repeat these 6 rows 2 (2, 3, 3) times—36 (40, 46, 50) stitches.

Knit 2 rows.

Decrease Row (Right Side) K2, ssk, knit to last 4 stitches, k2tog, k2.

Next Row P2, knit to last 2 stitches, p2.

Repeat last 2 rows 9 more times—16 (20, 26, 30) stitches.

Decrease Row K2, ssk, knit to last 4 stitches, k2tog, k2.
Next Row P2, k2tog, knit to last 4 stitches, k2tog, p2.

Repeat the last 2 rows 0 (1, 2, 3) times—12 (14, 14, 16) stitches.

Knit 2 rows.

Bind off.

DIAPER COVER FRONT

Work the same as for the Back.

DIAPER COVER FINISHING

Lightly steam-block the pieces. Sew Front and Back together along sides and crotch. Weave in ends. Beginning and ending at the center of the Front, thread ribbon through the Eyelet Row.

SUMMER BEACH CREEPER

A summer baby needs a knitted wardrobe, too. Knit in a lightweight cotton, this summer beach creeper is a perfect choice. Baby will look cool and feel comfortable when temperatures soar.

SKILL LEVEL
Intermediate

SIZES
0–6 months (12 months, 18 months, 24 months)

FINISHED MEASUREMENTS
Chest: 20 (22, 24½, 26)" (51 [56, 63.5, 66]cm)

Length: 13¾ (15½, 17, 18¼)" (35 [39.5, 43, 46.5]cm)

YARN
3 (4, 5, 6) balls of Rowan Handknit DK Cotton, 100% cotton, 1¾ oz (50g), 93 yd (85m) in #327 Aqua (A), (**4**) medium

1 ball of #326 Nectar (B)

NEEDLES AND NOTIONS
- US size 4 (3.5mm) knitting needles
- US size 5 (3.75mm) knitting needles, or size needed to obtain gauge
- Stitch holders
- Yarn needle
- 6 buttons, ½" (12mm) diameter

GAUGE
20 stitches and 28 rows = 4" (20cm) in stockinette stitch using larger needle

Adjust needle size as necessary to obtain correct gauge.

NOTES
1. The Creeper is worked in two pieces and sewn together along the side edges.
2. Each piece is worked from the crotch to the shoulder.
3. Short rows are used to add fullness to the Back.

SHORT ROWS
Wrap and turn: Bring yarn to the front, slip the next stitch as if to purl from the left-hand needle to the right-hand needle, turn work, wrap yarn around slipped stitch and slip same stitch back onto right-hand needle. On next row, work wrapped stitch by picking up wrap and working it together with the stitch on the left-hand needle.

STRIPE PATTERN
With A, work in stockinette stitch for 4 rows.

Change to B and knit 2 rows.

Repeat these 6 rows for Stripe Pattern.

BACK

Inseam
With A, cast on 13 (13, 15, 15) stitches.

Working in stockinette stitch, work 1 row.

Cast on 3 stitches at the beginning of the next 6 rows— 31 (31, 33, 33) stitches.

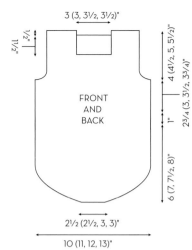

3 (3, 3½, 3½)"

1½"

½"

FRONT
AND
BACK

4 (4½, 5, 5½)"

2¾ (3, 3½, 3¾)"

1"

6 (7, 7½, 8)"

2½ (2½, 3, 3)"

10 (11, 12, 13)"

Cast on 2 stitches at the beginning of every row 10 (12, 14, 16) times—51 (55, 61, 65) stitches.

Continue in stockinette stitch until the piece measures 6 (7, 7½, 8)" (15 [18, 19, 20.5]cm) from the beginning, ending with a wrong-side row.

Shape Bottom (Short Rows)
Knit to last 5 stitches, wrap and turn.
Purl to last 5 stitches, wrap and turn.
Knit to last 10 stitches, wrap and turn.
Purl to last 10 stitches, wrap and turn.
Knit to last 15 stitches, wrap and turn.
Purl to last 15 stitches, wrap and turn.

Knit 1 row across all stitches, picking up and working the wraps.
Purl 1 row across all stitches.

Waist Rib
Change to smaller needles.

Row 1 (Right Side) K1, *p1, k1; repeat from * across.
Row 2 P1, *k1, p1; repeat from * across.

Repeat these 2 rows for 1" (2.5cm).

Top
With right side facing, change to larger needles and Stripe Pattern. Work until the piece measures 2¾ (3, 3½, 3¾)"

(7 [7.5, 9, 9.5]cm) from Waist Rib, ending with a wrong-side row.

Shape Armhole
Bind off 3 stitches at the beginning of the next 2 rows—45 (49, 56, 59) stitches.

Working in Stripe Pattern, decrease 1 stitch at each edge every row 4 times—41 (45, 51, 55) stitches.

Continue in Stripe Pattern until the armhole measures 3½ (4, 4½, 5)" (9 [10, 11.5, 12.5]cm), ending with a wrong-side row.

Shape Neck and Shoulders
With right side facing, work 13 (15, 17, 19) stitches and slip them to a stitch holder for the right shoulder, place next 15 (15, 17, 17) stitches on a stitch holder for neck, join a new ball of yarn, and work remaining 13 (15, 17, 19) stitches for the left shoulder.

Left Shoulder
Work in stripe pattern for 1½" (4cm). Bind off.

Right Shoulder
Slip stitches for right shoulder from stitch holder to needle and work in stripe pattern 4 rows. Place stitches on a stitch holder.

FRONT

Bottom
With A, cast on 13 (13, 15, 15) stitches.

Work in stockinette stitch for 1 row.

Cast on 3 stitches at the beginning of the next 6 rows—31 (31, 33, 33) stitches.

Cast on 2 stitches at the beginning of every row 10 (12, 14, 16) times—51 (55, 61, 65) stitches.

Continue in stockinette stitch until the piece measures 6 (7, 7½, 8)" (15 [18, 19, 20.5]cm) from the beginning, ending with a wrong-side row.

Waist Rib
Change to smaller needles.

Row 1 (Right Side) K1, *p1, k1; repeat from * across.
Row 2 P1, *k1, p1; repeat from * across.

Repeat these 2 rows for 1" (2.5cm).

Top
With right side facing, change to larger needles and Stripe Pattern. Work until the piece measures 2¾ (3, 3½, 3¾)" (7 [7.5, 9, 9.5]cm) from Waist Rib, ending with a wrong-side row.

Shape Armhole
Bind off 3 stitches at the beginning of the next 2 rows—45 (49, 56, 59) stitches.

Working in Stripe Pattern, decrease 1 stitch at each edge every row 4 times—41 (45, 51, 55) stitches. (On knit rows, k1, k2tog, knit to last 3 stitches, ssk, k1. On purl rows, p1, p2tog, purl to last 3 stitches, p2tog, p1.)

Continue in Stripe Pattern until the armhole measures 2 (2½, 3, 3½)" (5 [6.5, 7.5, 9]cm), ending with a wrong-side row.

Shape Neck and Shoulders
With right side facing, work 13 (15, 17, 19) stitches and slip them to a stitch holder for left shoulder, place next 15 (15, 17, 17) stitches on a stitch holder for neck, join a new ball of yarn, and work remaining 13 (15, 17, 19) stitches for the right shoulder.

Right Shoulder
Work in Stripe Pattern for 2" (5cm). Slip stitches to a stitch holder for shoulder.

Left Shoulder
Work in Stripe Pattern for 1½" (4cm), ending with a wrong-side row.

Buttonhole Row K2 (2, 3, 3), yo, k2tog, k2 (3, 3, 4), yo, k2tog, k2 (3, 3, 4), yo, k2tog, k1 (1, 2, 2).
Next Row Purl across.

Work 2 more rows in pattern.

Bind off.

FINISHING

Three-Needle Bind-Off
Place the Back right shoulder stitches on 1 needle. Matching the Front right shoulder stitches to Back right shoulder stitches, place

the Front right stitches on a second needle. Hold the pieces with right sides facing, and using a third needle and A, knit together 1 stitch each from Front and Back needles, and bind off. Continue to bind off the right shoulder stitches.

Neck Edging

With right side facing, smaller needles and A, join yarn at left shoulder at neck edge, pick up and knit 6 stitches along left Front neck edge, k15 (15, 17, 17) stitches from Front stitch holder, pick up and knit 6 from right Front neck edge, pick up 3 stitches from Back right shoulder, k15 (15, 17, 17) stitches from Back stitch holder, pick up and knit 10 stitches from left Back neck edge—55 (55, 59, 59) stitches. Do not join.

Row 1 P1, *k1, p1; repeat from * across.
Buttonhole Row (Right Side) K1, p1, yo, p2tog, work in rib across.

Work in rib for 2 more rows.

Bind off in pattern.

Armhole Edging

Overlap front left shoulder over back left shoulder 1" (2.5cm) at the armhole edge and sew in place for button band. Sew buttons opposite buttonholes.

With right side facing, smaller needles, and A, join yarn at underarm; pick up and knit 49 (57, 63, 69) stitches around the armhole. Work 1 row in stockinette stitch. Bind off.

Sew side seams.

Leg Edging

With right side facing and A, join yarn at crotch; pick up and knit 39 (43, 47, 51) stitches around the leg opening. Work in rib for 4 rows. Bind off.

Crotch Button Band

Back

With right side facing, pick up and knit 15 (15, 18, 18) stitches across the cast-on edge of the Back. Work in stockinette stitch for 4 rows. Bind off.

Front

With right side facing, pick up and knit 15 (15, 18, 18) stitches across the beginning cast-on edge of Front. Work in stockinette stitch for 3 rows.

Row 4 (Right Side) K4 (4, 5, 5), yo, k2tog, k3 (3, 4, 4), k2tog, yo, k4 (4, 5, 5).

Purl 1 row.

Bind off.

Sew buttons opposite buttonholes. Weave in ends. Lightly block.

The Name Game

ALMOST AS SOON AS YOU KNOW YOU'RE PREGNANT, YOU START THINKING ABOUT NAMES. How do you determine the "right" name for your baby? Do you go with trendy, unique, or family-inspired names? I would go to the park and listen to all the different names. If you called out the name Nora at the park, how many girls came running? I wanted a unique name. I was lucky, as Nora is also a family name—my mom's sister, my sister, and my dad's mother all are Nora. It was a perfect name.

I found picking the right boy name a bit more challenging. I had a few tests for my names.

1. No obvious nicknames (for example, James: Jimmy, Jim).

2. A nod to our heritage. My grandfather was named Coleman. This seemed too old for a little boy. We shortened it to Cole.

3. His monogram did not inadvertently spell anything. For example, Alan Stephen Smith or William Owen White.

To help you with your search, here are a few of the top names over the past decade. Favorite boy names according the US Social Security Administration are Jacob, Michael, Joshua, Matthew, Ethan, Andrew and Christopher. Favorite girl names include Emily, Emma, Madison, Ava, Olivia, Hannah and Ashley.

How about a few knitting-inspired ones, such as Lana, Pearl, Rowan, Kaffe, Elizabeth, Debbie, Lorna, Claudia, or Aran?

As much fun as the name game can be, it can also be very charged. You may associate names with school bullies from your childhood or old girlfriends and boyfriends. Extended family will also have their personal associations. My recommendation is just take name suggestions along with all the other advice you'll get in the next nine months with a smile.

BABY RACER SWEATER

This smart sweater is a perfect companion to the Baby Racer Leggings (page 70). The complementary colors will make it a versatile layer for any baby. The racing stripe shows off the beautiful hand-dyed yarns. Pair it with the leggings for an autumn stroll, or just throw on the sweater whenever there is a chill in the air.

SKILL LEVEL
Intermediate

SIZES
0–6 months (12 months, 18 months, 24 months)

FINISHED MEASUREMENTS
Chest: 20 (22, 24, 26)" (51 [56, 61, 66]cm)

Length: 10½ (12, 13, 14½)" (26.5 [30.5, 33, 37]cm)

YARN
4 (4, 5, 5) skeins of Artyarns Supermerino, 100% merino wool, 1¾ oz (50g), 104 yd (95m) in #SM22 Coral (A), (4) medium

1 skein in #SM141 Rose/Browns (B)

NEEDLES AND NOTIONS
- US size 6 (4mm) knitting needles, or size needed to obtain gauge
- US size 4 (3.5mm) knitting needles
- Yarn needle
- Stitch holders
- Bobbins
- 3 buttons, ½" (12mm) diameter

GAUGE
20 stitches and 24 rows = 4" (10cm) in stockinette stitch using larger needles

Adjust needle size as necessary to obtain correct gauge.

NOTES
1. The Back and Front are worked the same.
2. The racer stripe is worked in intarsia on each sleeve, using a different ball of yarn for each color change. Wind bobbins for each color. Remember to pick up the new color from under the old color to twist the yarns and prevent holes.

BACK
With smaller needles and A, cast on 50 (55, 60, 65) stitches.

Knit every row for ¾" (9.5cm), ending with a wrong-side row.

Changing to larger needles and stockinette stitch, work until the piece measures 6½ (7½, 8, 9)" (16.5 [19, 20.5, 23]cm) from the beginning, ending with a wrong-side row.

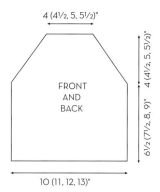

4 (4½, 5, 5½)"

4 (4½, 5, 5½)"

FRONT
AND
BACK

6½ (7½, 8, 9)"

10 (11, 12, 13)"

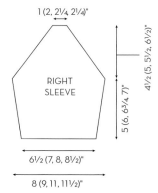

1 (2, 2¼, 2¼)"

RIGHT
SLEEVE

4½ (5, 5½, 6½)"

5 (6, 6¾, 7)"

6½ (7, 8, 8½)"

8 (9, 11, 11½)"

Shape Armhole

Bind off 3 stitches at the beginning of the next 2 rows.

Decrease Row (Right Side) K2, ssk, knit to last 4 stitches, k2tog, k2.
Purl 1 row.

Repeat these last 2 rows 11 (12, 14, 15) more times—20 (23, 24, 27) stitches. Place these stitches on a holder.

FRONT

Work the same as for the Back.

RIGHT SLEEVE

With smaller needles and B, cast on 33 (35, 39, 43) stitches.

Knit every row for ¾" (9.5cm), ending with a wrong-side row.

Change to larger needles and stockinette stitch.
Next Row (Right Side) K14 (15, 17, 19) with A, k5 with B, k14 (15, 17, 19) with A.
Continue to work in stockinette stitch, working the center 5 stitches with B.

AT THE SAME TIME, increase 1 stitch at each edge every fourth row as follows:
Row 1 Purl.
Row 2 Knit.
Row 3 Purl.
Row 4 K1, M1, knit to last stitch, M1, k1. Work these 4 rows 3 (5, 6, 6) times—39 (45, 51, 55) stitches.

Continue until the Sleeve measures 5 (6, 6¾, 7)" (12.5 [15,

17, 18]cm) from the beginning, ending with a wrong-side row.

Shape Armhole

Bind off 3 stitches at the beginning of the next 2 rows—33 (39, 45, 49) stitches.

Decrease Row (Right Side) K2, ssk, knit to last 4 stitches, k2tog, k2.
Purl 1 row.

Repeat these last 2 rows 13 (14, 16, 18) more times—5 (9, 11, 11) stitches. Place these stitches on a holder.

LEFT SLEEVE

With smaller needles and B, cast on 33 (35, 39, 43) stitches.

Knit every row for ¾" (9.5cm), ending with a wrong-side row.

Change to larger needles and stockinette stitch.
Next Row (Right Side) K14 (15, 17, 19) with A, k5 with B, k14 (15, 17, 19) with A.

Continue to work in stockinette stitch, working the center 5 stitches with B.

AT THE SAME TIME, increase 1 stitch at each edge every fourth row as follows:
Row 1 Purl.
Row 2 Knit.
Row 3 Purl.
Row 4 K1, M1, knit to last stitch, M1, k1.
Work these 4 rows 3 (5, 6, 6) times—39 (45, 51, 55) stitches.

Continue until the Sleeve measures 5 (6, 6¾, 7)" (12.5 [15, 17, 18]cm) from the beginning, ending with a wrong-side row.

Shape Armhole

Bind off 3 stitches at the beginning of the next 2 rows—33 (39, 45, 49) stitches.

Decrease Row (Right Side) K2, ssk, knit to last 4 stitches, k2tog, k2.
Next Row Cast on 3 stitches, purl to end.
Decrease Row (Right Side) K2, ssk, knit to last 7 stitches, k2tog, k5.

Repeat these last 2 rows 12 (13, 16, 17) more times—5 (9, 11, 11) stitches. Place these stitches on a holder.

FINISHING

Lightly block.

Sew Right Sleeve into raglan armhole shaping of Front and Back. Sew Left Sleeve into raglan armhole shaping of Back. Sew side and sleeve seams.

Neck Band

With right side facing, smaller needles, and B, k5 (9, 11, 11) from Right Sleeve stitch holder, k20 (23, 24, 27) stitches from Back stitch holder, k5 (9, 11, 11) stitches from Left Sleeve stitch holder— 30 (41, 46, 49) stitches.

Knit 4 rows. Bind off loosely.

Matching Baby Racer Leggings are found on page 70.

Buttonhole Band

With right side facing, smaller needles, and B, join yarn at left armhole of Front and pick up and knit 20 (24, 28, 30) stitches from the raglan armhole shaping, k20 (23, 24, 27) stitches from Front stitch holder—40 (47, 52, 57) stitches.

Knit 3 rows.

Buttonhole Row (Right Side) K3 (4, 5, 7), *yo, k2tog, k3 (4, 5, 5); repeat from * twice more, knit to end.
Knit 2 rows. Bind off.

Sew buttons opposite buttonholes. Sew the edges of the buttonhole band and neck band together at the Left Sleeve.

Weave in ends.

BABY RACER LEGGINGS

Knit in a machine-washable yarn, these pants are a perfect way to wrap your little darling up for a stroll in the autumn air, and there is no need to worry about spills or spit-up. The matching Baby Racer Sweater (page 66), with a racing stripe down the sleeve, creates a warm and stylish outfit.

SKILL LEVEL
Intermediate

SIZES
0–6 months (12 months, 18 months, 24 months)

FINISHED MEASUREMENTS
Waist: 13 (15, 18, 20)" (33 [38, 45.5, 51]cm)

Length: 16 (18, 21, 23)" (40.5 [45.5, 53.5, 58.5]cm)

YARN
3 (4, 4, 5) skeins of Artyarns Supermerino, 100% merino wool, 1¾ oz (50g), 104 yd (95m) in #SM141 Rose/Browns, (4) medium

NEEDLES AND NOTIONS
- US size 6 (4mm) knitting needles, or size needed to obtain gauge
- US size 4 (3.5mm) knitting needles
- Yarn needle

GAUGE
20 stitches and 24 rows = 4" (10cm) in stockinette stitch using larger needles.

Adjust needle size as necessary to obtain correct gauge.

NOTES
1. The Leggings are knit in two pieces, back and forth in rows, from the waist down to the cuff. The Legs are sewn together at the center waist.
2. Short rows are used to add fullness to the back.
3. Short row shaping is used to add an approximate 1½" (4cm) rise to the back of the pants. Take care when measuring for length measurements. All measurements should be taken from the center of the piece.

SHORT ROWS
Wrap and turn: Bring yarn to front, slip next stitch, turn, wrap yarn around slip stitch and slip same stitch back onto right-hand needle. On next round, work wrapped stitch by picking up wrap and working together with the stitch on the left-hand needle.

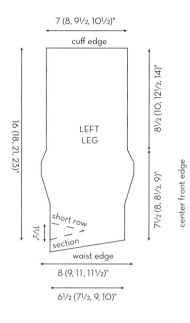

Diagram labels: 7 (8, 9½, 10½)" — cuff edge — LEFT LEG — 8½ (10, 12½, 14)" — 16 (18, 21, 23)" — 7½ (8, 8½, 9)" — center front edge — short row section — 1½" — waist edge — 8 (9, 11, 11½)" — 6½ (7½, 9, 10)"

RIGHT PANT LEG

Waistband

Using smaller needles, cast on 32 (38, 46, 50) stitches.

Row 1 *K1, p1; repeat from * across.

Repeat row 1 for ribbing until piece measures ¾ (1, 1, 1)" (2 [2.5, 2.5, 2.5]cm) from the beginning, ending with a wrong-side row.

Change to larger needles and stockinette stitch, and work 2 rows.

Back Shaping (Short Rows)

K5, wrap and turn.
P5, wrap and turn.

K10, wrap and turn.
P10, wrap and turn.

K15, wrap and turn.
P15, wrap and turn.

K20, wrap and turn.
P20, wrap and turn.

Continue in stockinette stitch across all the stitches until the piece measures 2 (3, 3½, 4)" (5 [7.5, 9, 10]cm) from ribbing, ending with a wrong-side row.

Increase Row (Right Side) K1, m1, knit to last stitch, m1, k1.
Work 3 rows even.

Repeat last 4 rows 4 times—40 (46, 54, 58) stitches.

Work even until the piece measures 6½ (7, 7½, 8)" (16.5 [18, 19, 20.5]cm) from the beginning, ending with a wrong-side row.

Shape Leg

Next Row (Right Side) K1, ssk, knit to last 3 stitches, k2tog, k1. Purl 1 row.

Repeat the last 2 rows twice more—34 (40, 48, 52) stitches.

Continue until the piece measures 16 (18, 21, 23)" (40.5 [45.5, 53.5, 58.5]cm) from the beginning. Bind off loosely.

LEFT PANT LEG

Waistband

Using smaller needles, cast on 32 (38, 46, 50) stitches.

Row 1 *K1, p1; repeat from * across.

Repeat row 1 for ribbing until piece measures ¾ (1, 1, 1)" (2 [2.5, 2.5, 2.5]cm) from the beginning, ending with a wrong-side row.

Change to larger needles and stockinette stitch, and work 3 rows.

Back Shaping (Short Rows)

P5, wrap and turn.
K5, wrap and turn.

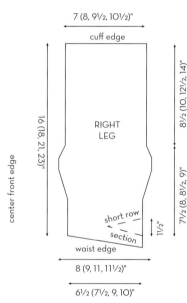

Diagram labels: 7 (8, 9½, 10½)" — cuff edge — RIGHT LEG — 8½ (10, 12½, 14)" — 16 (18, 21, 23)" — center front edge — 7½ (8, 8½, 9)" — short row section — 1½" — waist edge — 8 (9, 11, 11½)" — 6½ (7½, 9, 10)"

P10, wrap and turn.
K10, wrap and turn.

P15, wrap and turn.
K15, wrap and turn.

P20, wrap and turn.
K20, wrap and turn.

Continue in stockinette stitch across all stitches until the piece measures 2 (3, 3½, 4)" (5 [7.5, 9, 10]cm) from ribbing, ending with a wrong-side row.

Increase Row (Right Side) K1, m1, knit to last stitch, m1, k1.
Work 3 rows even.

Repeat last 4 rows 4 times—40 (46, 54, 58) stitches.

Work even until the piece measures 6½ (7, 7½, 8)" (16.5 [18, 19, 20.5]cm) from the beginning, ending with a wrong-side row.

Shape Leg

Next Row (Right Side) K1, ssk, knit to last 3 stitches, k2tog, k1.
Purl 1 row.

Repeat the last 2 rows twice more—34 (40, 48, 52) stitches.

Continue until the piece measures 16 (18, 21, 23)" (40.5 [45.5, 53.5, 58.5]cm) from the beginning. Bind off loosely.

FINISHING

Lightly block. Sew the Legs together along the center of the front and back seams. Sew the Leg seams. Weave in ends.

ALPHABET BLOCK TOYS

A, B, C . . . baby's first alphabet blocks, easy as 1, 2, 3! Knit in soft cotton, these blocks are just right for small hands. They can be washed and played with over and over again.

SKILL LEVEL
Intermediate

FINISHED MEASUREMENTS
4" (10cm) cube

YARN
1 ball each of Rowan Handknit DK Cotton, 100% cotton, 1¾ oz (50g), 93 yd (85m) in #327 Aqua (A), #254 Flame (B), #215 Rosso (C), #324 Bermuda (D), and #303 Sugar (E), medium

NEEDLES AND NOTIONS
- US size 5 (3.75mm) knitting needles, or size needed to obtain gauge
- Bobbins
- Yarn needle
- Polyester fiber filling

GAUGE
20 stitches and 28 rows = 4" (20cm) in stockinette stitch

Adjust needle size as necessary to obtain correct gauge.

NOTES:
1. The Squares are worked in intarsia, using a different ball of yarn for each color change. Wind bobbins for each color.
2. Pick up the new color from under the old color to twist the yarns and prevent holes.
3. Four cubes consist of five squares with letters and one blank square. The fifth cube consists of six squares with letters.

LETTER SQUARES (MAKE 26)
With main color, cast on 20 stitches. Working in stockinette stitch, follow the charts on pages 76 and 77 (one for each letter) to work 28 rows. Bind off.

BLANK SQUARES (MAKE 4)
With main color, cast on 20 stitches. Work in stockinette stitch for 28 rows. Bind off.

FINISHING
Weave in ends. Steam-block the pieces.

Following assembly diagrams, sew 5 squares with letters and 1 blank square together to make a cube. Leave one side open for stuffing, and stuff with fiber filling. Sew the remaining side closed.

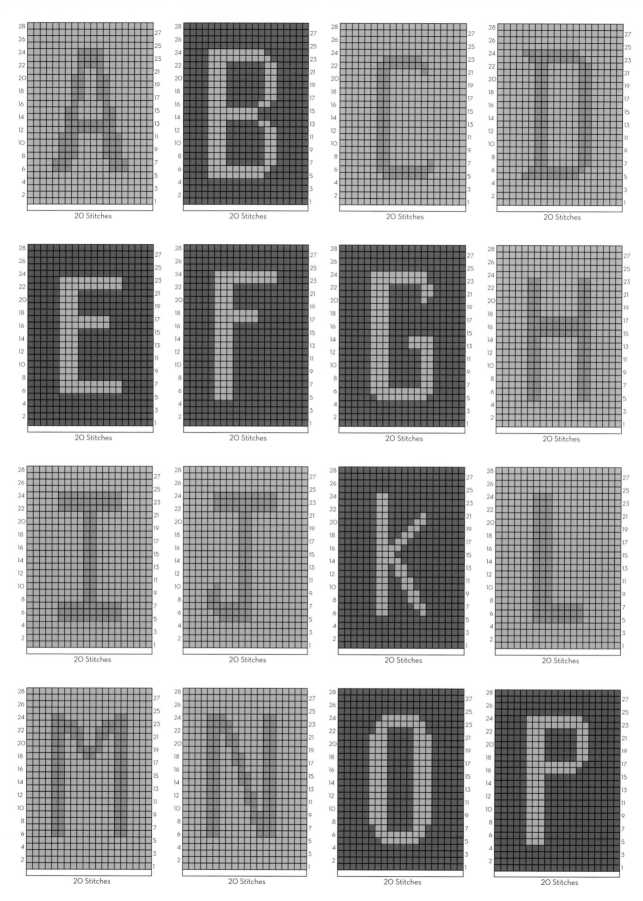

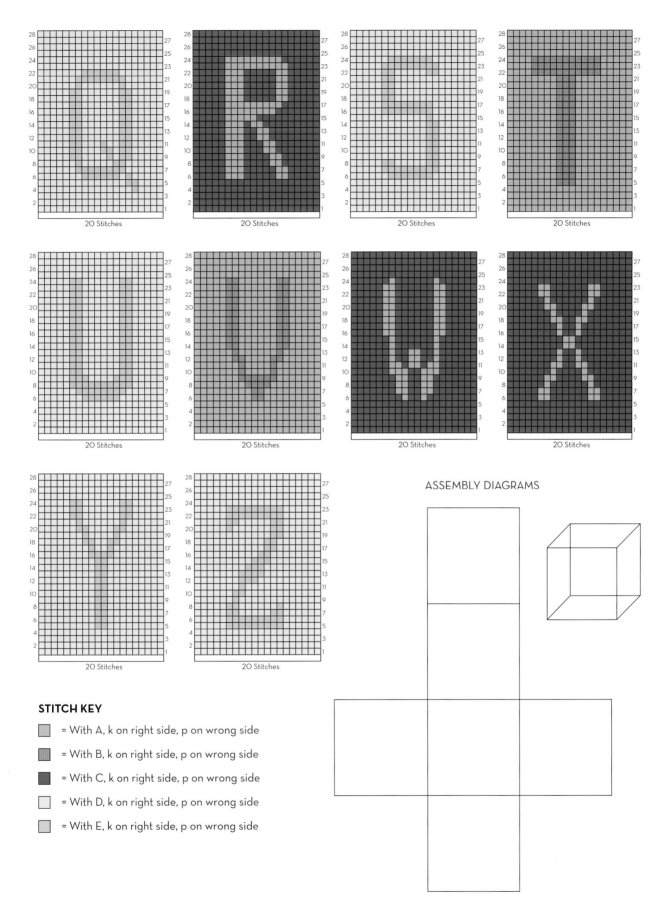

ASSEMBLY DIAGRAMS

STITCH KEY

[A] = With A, k on right side, p on wrong side

[B] = With B, k on right side, p on wrong side

[C] = With C, k on right side, p on wrong side

[D] = With D, k on right side, p on wrong side

[E] = With E, k on right side, p on wrong side

Feel the Energy, Spread the Love!

IF YOU HAVE BEEN KEEPING QUIET, it's now time to shout, "I'm pregnant!" Your morning sickness should be coming to an end. You may feel what many call the "second trimester surge." Enjoy the extra energy.

Take this time as your bump is growing to prime the rest of the family for the impending delivery. Start some bigger knitting projects. Many of this chapter's projects shift your attention to the rest of the family—Dad, soon-to-be older siblings, and even the family dog. Use some of your extra energy to knit, and spend some special one-on-one time with your husband and kids. Just don't push yourself too hard. Listen to your body. Take breaks, and savor midday naps, as they will be harder to get once the baby arrives.

Yes, everything changes with the arrival of a new baby. Saturday morning routines change from coffee in bed reading the paper to breastfeeding in bed, folding baby clothes, and hoping that the dog doesn't shred the

neglected newspaper. Remember, change can be good. Embrace the changes, and look to the future with hope, because without these changes you wouldn't get to experience your baby's first smile, first words, first steps.

Before the baby arrives, take some important steps to get the household ready. I'm not talking about the traditional baby-proofing of the house but rather baby-proofing your husband, older kids, and pets. Along with the knitted projects, I include some helpful tips for preparing your family for the new baby's arrival. Use the projects and the tips to make the changes a little less challenging for everyone. I'm sure Dad will really enjoy the cashmere socks. Who wouldn't? He may even enjoy the nighttime feedings when he's wearing them! The Big Sister Sweater (page 90) and the Big Brother Hooded Sweater (page 94) are simple to knit but perfect gifts for the older siblings to open when all the new baby gifts start to arrive.

Second Trimester

Week 14: As your belly grows, the clothing choices may be shrinking. Raid your husband's closet for some oversized tops, or get going on the cashmere Shawl Sweater (page 117).

Week 15: Embrace your changing body—consider taking weekly pictures of your enlarging belly.

Week 16: If you're having an amniocentesis, it's best to schedule it for the coming 2-4 weeks.

Week 17: Your baby is growing and now measures five inches long and weighs half an ounce.

Week 18: Those flutters may not be gas. You'll start to feel baby movements in the next 4 weeks.

Week 19: Time to schedule your sonogram. Now you can learn if you are knitting for a boy or a girl.

Week 20: Start spreading the news—although your bump may have spoiled the secret already.

Week 21: Eating for two? Remember that calories count. Make healthy eating choices and instead just knit for two.

Week 22: Disposable or reusable? You'll possibly change between 4,000 to 5,000 diapers over the next three years. Explore the many possibilities. Whatever you choose, knit a couple of wool diaper covers (page 108).

Week 23: What about Daddy? Put down your knitting tonight and have a date night. It may be months before you have another.

Week 24: How does your baby grow? She's about 8 inches long and almost 1 pound.

Week 25: Time to set up your baby-shower registry. Consider registering at your local yarn shop for knitting items! Pick out colors, fibers, and patterns that your friends and family can select from.

Week 26: Ask friends and family for pediatrician recommendations.

Week 27: Make something special for Dad—check out the easy socks on page 87. Who knows, you might even make a second pair for yourself. Remember, you don't have to be barefoot when pregnant!

SHAWL COLLAR SWEATER

This sweater is a special one that I knit for my son, Cole. It was fashioned after a sweater that I'd love to knit for my husband, but I just haven't gotten around to it. So, I figured I'd test out the pattern, which features a generous cowl collar made in a baby version, with the softest merino.

SKILL LEVEL
Intermediate

SIZES
0–6 months (12 months, 18 months, 24 months)

FINISHED MEASUREMENTS
Chest: 20 (22, 25, 26)" (51 [56, 63.5, 66]cm)

Length: 9½ (11, 12, 13)" (24 [28, 30.5, 33]cm)

YARN
3 (4, 4, 5) skeins of Pear Tree 8-Ply Merino, 100% Australian merino wool, 1¾ oz (50g), 107 yd (98m) in Moss, (**4**) medium

NEEDLES AND NOTIONS
- US size 6 (4mm) knitting needles, or size needed to obtain gauge
- US size 4 (3.5mm) knitting needles
- Stitch holders
- Locking stitch markers
- Yarn needle

GAUGE
22 stitches and 28 rows = 4" (10cm) in stockinette stitch using the larger needle

Adjust needle size as necessary to obtain correct gauge.

NOTE
The sweater features a garter stitch border that runs along the bottom and up 2" (5cm) on the sides of both the Front and Back.

ABBREVIATIONS
K2tog: This is an easy right-slanting decrease. Knit the next two stitches at the same time.

Ssk: (A slightly more advanced decrease that slants left. Worked with the K2tog, it will produce a mirrored decrease that will make your garments look very professional.) Slip the next two stitches individually knitwise from the left-hand needle to the right-hand needle as if to knit. Then place the left-hand needle into these two stitches through the front loops and, using your right-hand needle, which is now in the back loops of these stitches, knit them together.

SHORT ROWS
Wrap and turn: Bring yarn to front, slip next stitch, turn, wrap yarn around slip stitch and slip same stitch back onto the right-hand needle. On the next row, work wrapped stitch by picking up wrap and working together

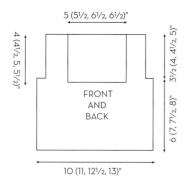

FRONT AND BACK

5 (5½, 6½, 6½)"

4 (4½, 5, 5½)"

3½ (4, 4½, 5)"

6 (7, 7½, 8)"

10 (11, 12½, 13)"

SLEEVE

7 (8, 9, 10)"

7½ (8½, 9, 9½)"

with the stitch on the left-hand needle.

BACK

With larger needles, cast on 55 (61, 69, 73) stitches.

Knit 8 rows.

Change to stockinette stitch, knitting the first and last 3 stitches of every row, until the garment measures 2" (5cm) from the beginning.

Work in stockinette stitch on all stitches until the piece measures 6 (7, 7½, 8)" (16 [18, 19, 20.5]cm) from the beginning, ending with a wrong-side row.

Shape Armholes
Bind off 4 stitches at the beginning of the next 2 rows— 47 (53, 61, 65) stitches.

Work in stockinette stitch until the armhole measures 3½ (4, 4½, 5)" (9 [10, 11.5, 12.5]cm)

Shape Neck and Shoulders
With right side facing, k9 (11, 13, 15) stitches and slip stitches to a stitch holder for shoulder, bind off center 29 (31, 35, 35) stitches for neck, and k9 (11, 13, 15) stitches and slip stitches to a stitch holder for shoulder.

FRONT

With larger needles, cast on 55 (61, 69, 73) stitches.

Knit 8 rows.

Work in stockinette stitch, knitting the first 3 and last 3 stitches of every row, until the garment measures 2" (5cm) from the beginning.

Work in stockinette stitch on all stitches until the piece measures 5½ (6½, 7, 7½)" (14 [16.5, 18, 19]cm) from the beginning, ending with a wrong-side row.

Shape Neck and Shoulders
With right side facing, k16 (18, 20, 22) stitches and slip to a stitch holder for left shoulder, bind off center 23 (25, 29, 29) stitches for neck, and k16 (18, 20, 22) stitches for right shoulder. Work shoulders separately.

Right Shoulder
Purl 1 row.
Decrease Row K1, ssk, knit across. Work 2 rows.
Next Row (Wrong Side) Bind off 4 stitches, purl across.

Work Decrease Row every fourth row twice more—9 (11, 13, 15) stitches. Work until the Front measures same length as the Back to the shoulders. Slip stitches to a stitch holder.

Left Shoulder
Slip stitches from stitch holder to needle, join yarn on wrong side, and purl 1 row.

DaDaDaDa

ALAN AND I HAD A LONG HONEYMOON BEFORE OUR FIRST CHILD, NORA, ARRIVED. We had three years to fine-tune our routines before they were shattered by our new baby. As I was expecting Cole, I wanted to make a sweater for Alan. Once I learned I was having a boy, I decided I would test out a baby version of the pattern, which is now the Shawl Collar Sweater (page 82). Alan can't wait to get his sweater soon!

Remember, even though you may be feeling bloated, scared, and tired, Daddy has feelings, too. Talk to him. Share your hopes and fears. If you have older kids, call a sitter and go on a date together. Go for walks together. You have to feed your relationship. And if you have time, knit him something small and sweet like the cashmere Warm Toes, Warm Heart Socks on page 87.

Decrease Row Knit to last 2 stitches, k2tog.
Work 1 row.
Next Row (Right Side) Bind off 4 stitches, knit across.

Work Decrease Row every fourth row twice more—9 (11, 13, 15) stitches. Work until the Front measures same length as the Back to the shoulders. Slip stitches to a stitch holder.

SLEEVES (MAKE 2)
With larger needles, cast on 33 (37, 39, 43) stitches.

Knit for 8 rows.

Change to stockinette stitch and work 6 rows.
Increase Row (Right Side) K2, M1, knit to last 2 stitches, M1, k2.

Repeat Increase Row every 8 (6, 6, 6) rows 2 (3, 5, 5) times more—39 (45, 51, 55) stitches.

Work until the sleeve measures 7½ (8½, 9, 9½)" (19 [21.5, 23, 24]cm) from the beginning. Bind off.

Work in pattern for 28 stitches, wrap and turn.
Work in pattern for 32 stitches, wrap and turn.

Continue to work short rows as established, working 4 more stitches on each turn, until all stitches have been worked.

Work 1 row across all stitches, picking up and working the wraps as you come to them. Bind off in pattern.

FINISHING

Three-Needle Bind-Off

Place the Back right shoulder stitches on 1 needle. Matching the Front right shoulder stitches to the Back right shoulder stitches, place the Front right stitches on a second needle. Hold the pieces with right sides facing, and, using a third needle and A, knit together 1 stitch each from Front and Back needles, and bind off. Continue to bind off the right shoulder stitches.

Sew Sleeves into armholes. Sew the side and sleeve seams, leaving garter stitch borders open as side vents. Sew Collar into neck. Weave in ends. Lightly block.

SHAWL COLLAR

Cast on 104 (112, 128, 140) stitches.

Row 1 (Wrong Side) P3, *k2, p2; repeat from * to last 5 stitches, k2, p3.
Row 2 K3, *p2, k2; repeat from * to last 5 stitches, p2, k3.

Repeat last 2 rows until the collar measures 4½ (4½, 5½, 5½)" (11.5 [11.5, 14, 14]cm) from the beginning.

Collar Shaping (Short Rows)

Work in pattern for 60 (64, 72, 78) stitches, wrap and turn.
Work in pattern for 16 stitches, wrap and turn.
Work in pattern for 20 stitches, wrap and turn.
Work in pattern for 24 stitches, wrap and turn.

WARM TOES, WARM HEART SOCKS

Knit in the softest cashmere, these socks will warm Daddy's toes. He'll love wearing them to work, to bed, or just about anytime he wants to feel the love.

SKILL LEVEL
Intermediate

SIZE
Men's Medium (US size 9–11)

FINISHED MEASUREMENTS
Ankle Circumference: 9¾" (25cm)

Foot Length: 9½" (24cm)

YARN
1 skein of Jade Sapphire 4-ply Mongolian Cashmere, 100% cashmere, 2 oz (55g), 200 yd (183m) in #019 Robin's Egg Blue, **2** fine

NEEDLES AND NOTIONS
- US size 3 (3.25mm) double-pointed knitting needles
- US size 6 (4.00mm) double-pointed knitting needles or size needed to obtain gauge
- Stitch markers
- Yarn needle

GAUGE
26 stitches and 38 rows = 4" (10cm) in stockinette stitch using larger needles

Adjust needle size as necessary to obtain correct gauge.

NOTES
1. The Socks are worked in the round on double-pointed knitting needles from the cuff to the toe.
2. Short rows are used to create the heel.
3. The toe stitches are grafted together.

SHORT ROWS
Wrap and turn: Bring yarn to front, slip next stitch, turn, wrap yarn around slip stitch and slip same stitch back onto the right-hand needle. On the next row, work wrapped stitch by picking up wrap and working together with the stitch on the left-hand needle.

CUFF
With smaller needles, cast on 60 stitches and divide evenly among needles. Join to work in the round, being careful not to twist the stitches; place a marker for the beginning of the round.

Round 1 *K2, p1; repeat from * around.

Work 3 rounds.

Change to larger needles and work until cuff measures 3½" (8cm) from cast on edge. Change back to smaller needles and start the Heel.

HEEL

K30, wrap and turn.

P30, wrap and turn.

K29, wrap and turn.

P28, wrap and turn.

K27, wrap and turn.

P26, wrap and turn.

K25, wrap and turn.

P24, wrap and turn.

K23, wrap and turn.

P22, wrap and turn.

K21, wrap and turn.

P20, wrap and turn.

K19, wrap and turn.

P18, wrap and turn.

K17, wrap and turn.

P16, wrap and turn.

K15, wrap and turn.

P14, wrap and turn.

K13, wrap and turn.

P12, wrap and turn.

K11, wrap and turn.

P10, wrap and turn.

K11, wrap and turn.

P12, wrap and turn.

K13, wrap and turn.

P14, wrap and turn.

K15, wrap and turn.

P16, wrap and turn.
K17, wrap and turn.
P18, wrap and turn.
K19, wrap and turn.
P20, wrap and turn.
K21, wrap and turn.
P22, wrap and turn.
K23, wrap and turn.
P24, wrap and turn.
K25, wrap and turn.
P26, wrap and turn.
K27, wrap and turn.
P28, wrap and turn.
K29, wrap and turn.
P30, wrap and turn.

Place marker for beginning of round, knit 30, place marker, knit remaining stitches.

Work in stockinette stitch in the round on all the stitches until the sock measures 6¼" (16cm) from the tip of the Heel.

TOE
Round 1 *K1, k2tog, knit to marker, ssk, k1; repeat from * around.
Round 2 Knit.

Repeat last 2 rounds 11 more times—12 stitches remain.

Graft Toe Stitches
Divide remaining stitches between 2 needles and hold needles parallel to each other.

1. Thread yarn needle with yarn.
2. Set up stitches: Put the yarn needle into the first stitch on the front knitting needle as if to purl, and pull the yarn through. Next, pull the yarn needle through the first stitch on the rear knitting needle as if to knit.
3. Pull the yarn needle through the first stitch on the front knitting needle again as if to knit, and slip the stitch off the knitting needle. Next, pull yarn needle through the second stitch on the front knitting needle as if to purl, but leave this stitch on the knitting needle.
4. Pull the yarn needle through the first stitch on the rear knitting needle as if to purl, and slip the stitch off the knitting needle. Next, pull the yarn needle through the second stitch on the rear knitting needle as if to knit, but leave this stitch on the knitting needle.

Repeat Steps 3 and 4 until all stitches have been worked.

FINISHING
Weave in ends. Lightly block.

BIG SISTER SWEATER

Sugar and spice and everything nice, that's what the Big Sister Sweater is made of. Knit in the softest 4-ply cashmere in Nora's favorite color, this sweater was a joy to make. With little or no shaping and minimal finishing, it can be knit in just a weekend. It knits up so quickly, you might even make a second!

SKILL LEVEL
Beginner

SIZES
2 years (4 years, 6 years, 8 years)

FINISHED MEASUREMENTS
Chest: 23 (26, 27, 28)" (58.5 [66, 68.5, 71]cm)

Length: 9½ (12, 13½, 15)" (24 [30.5, 34.5, 38]cm)

YARN
2 (2, 3, 3) skeins of Jade Sapphire 4-ply Mongolian Cashmere, 100% cashmere, 2 oz (55g), 200 yd (183m) in #022 Little Girl Pink, fine

NEEDLES AND NOTIONS
- US size 5 (3.75mm) knitting needles
- US size 7 (4.5mm) knitting needles, or size needed to obtain gauge
- Yarn needle

GAUGE
24 stitches and 32 rows = 4" (10cm) in stockinette stitch using larger needles

Adjust needle size as necessary to obtain correct gauge.

NOTE
Front and Back are worked the same.

BACK
With smaller needles, cast on 70 (78, 82, 86) stitches.

Row 1 (Wrong Side) P2, *k2, p2; repeat from * across.
Row 2 (Right Side) K2, *p2, k2; repeat from * across.

Repeat rows 1 and 2 until the piece measures 1½ (2, 2, 2)" (4 [5, 5, 5]cm) from the beginning, ending with a wrong-side row.

Change to larger needles and stockinette stitch, and work until the piece measures 5½ (7½, 8½, 9½)" (14 [19, 21.5, 24]cm) from the beginning, ending with a wrong-side row.

Shape Armhole
Bind off 4 stitches at the beginning of the next 2 rows—62 (70, 74, 78) stitches.

I Thought I Was the Baby

NORA WAS AN ONLY CHILD FOR SIX AND A HALF YEARS. Yes, we doted on our only child. She was shocked to learn that a new brother or sister was on the way. She wasn't angry or scared but rather excited and concerned. She was old enough to know things would change but still naive enough to believe that they wouldn't. Here are some tips to consider as you prepare your kids for a new arrival.

1. *Talk to your children.* Tell them what's happening. But don't tell them before you want everyone else to know. We told Nora very early in my pregnancy. We had hoped to keep our family secret under wraps for a few more weeks. But with Nora's excitement came very loose lips. She was at the store one weekend and announced to everyone who walked in that I was indeed having a baby.

2. *Carve out non-baby time even before the baby arrives.* Find things to do together that are special for your older child. For Nora, it was as simple as walking her to school every day. She and I would chat along the way. I also knit a special sweater in pretty pink cashmere just for her. She picked out the yarn, and I probably gave in out of guilt. The Big Sister Sweater is soft, the pattern is extremely easy, and the cashmere, well, it is absolutely wonderful to knit. Make it yourself; the pattern starts on page 90.

3. *Enlist advice in preparing for the baby.* As you select nursery themes, baby names, or knitting yarns, ask your children for help. Nora helped select Cole's name.

4. *Prepare a sibling kit for the big day.* As you start to prepare your hospital bag, also prepare a sibling bag. Toss in some card games, a camera, reading and activity books, crayons, paper, and, if he or she is old enough, a knitting project.

5. *Remind the rest of the family of the older sibling's feelings.* It's very easy to overlook the older child when a new baby comes into the picture. Schedule some special private time with the grandparents, if possible, for your older child.

6. *Relax.* Kids are resilient. Your fears melted with the first smile. In time, so will theirs.

Continue in stockinette stitch until the piece measures 8 (10, 11½, 13)" (20.5 [25.5, 29, 33]cm) from the beginning, ending with a wrong-side row. Change to smaller needles.

Row 1 (Right Side) K2, *p2, k2; repeat from * across.
Row 2 (Wrong Side) P2, *k2, p2; repeat from * across.

Repeat rows 1 and 2 for 1½ (2, 2, 2)" (4 [5, 5, 5]cm). Bind off in pattern.

FRONT
Work as for the Back.

SLEEVES (MAKE 2)
With smaller needles, cast on 30 (38, 42, 50) stitches.

Row 1 (Wrong Side) P2, *k2, p2; repeat from * across.
Row 2 (Right Side) K2, *p2, k2; repeat from * across.

Repeat rows 1 and 2 until the Sleeve measures 1½ (2, 2, 2)" (4 [5, 5, 5]cm), ending with a wrong-side row.

Change to larger needles and stockinette stitch, increasing 1 stitch each edge every 4 (4, 4, 6) rows 9 (8, 9, 8) times as follows:

With the wrong side facing, start stockinette stitch (purl the first row), and work for 3 (3, 3, 5) rows.

Increase Row K1, k1f&b, knit to the last 2 stitches, k1f&b, k1— 48 (54, 60, 66) stitches.

Work even in stockinette stitch until the Sleeve measures 6½ (8½, 9½, 10½)" (16.5 [21.5, 24, 26.5]cm).

Bind off.

FINISHING
Sew the shoulders together, leaving 5 (6, 6½, 7)" (12.5 [15 16.5, 18]cm) in the center unsewn for neck. Adjust the neck opening for desired fit.

Sew Sleeves into armholes. Sew side and sleeve seams. Weave in ends. Lightly block.

BIG BROTHER HOODED SWEATER

This simple hoodie is made with four easily knit pieces. In machine-washable wool and classic colors, this sweater will be a hit with every soon-to-be big brother. It also will become a perfect hand-me-down when little brother grows up.

SKILL LEVEL
Beginner

SIZES
2 years (4 years, 6 years, 8 years)

FINISHED MEASUREMENTS
Chest: 24 (27, 28, 29)" (61 [68.5, 71, 73.5]cm)

Length: 15 (15½, 17½, 21)" (38 [39.5, 44.5, 53.5]cm)

YARN
8 (9, 10, 12) balls of Mission Falls 1824 Wool, 100% superwash merino wool, 1¾ oz (50g), 84 yd (77m) in #022 Ink (A), (4) medium

1 ball in #013 Curry (B)

1 (1, 1, 2) balls in #532 Basil (C)

NEEDLES AND NOTIONS
- US size 7 (4.5mm) knitting needles
- US size 8 (5mm) knitting needles, or size needed to obtain gauge
- Yarn needle

GAUGE
16 stitches and 24 rows = 4" (10cm) in stockinette stitch

Adjust needle size as necessary to obtain correct gauge.

NOTE
The Sweater is composed of simple rectangle shapes with minimal shaping details. The Front and Back are worked the same. The Sleeves are extended to include the Front and Back shoulders and are joined at the center of the Body.

BACK
With smaller knitting needles and A, cast on 48 (54, 56 58) stitches.

Work in garter stitch for 1" (2.5cm), ending with a wrong-side row.

Change to larger needles and stockinette stitch and work until the piece measures 4½ (5, 6 7½)" (11.5 [12.5, 15, 19]cm) from the beginning, ending with a wrong-side row.

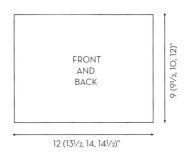

FRONT
AND
BACK

9 (9½, 10, 12)"

12 (13½, 14, 14½)"

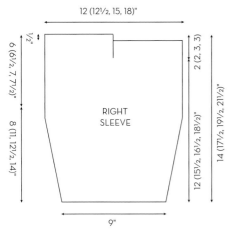

12 (12½, 15, 18)"

½"

6 (6½, 7, 7½)"

8 (11, 12½, 14)"

RIGHT
SLEEVE

2 (2, 3, 3)"

12 (15½, 16½, 18½)"

14 (17½, 19½, 21½)"

9"

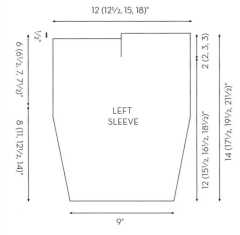

12 (12½, 15, 18)"

½"

6 (6½, 7, 7½)"

8 (11, 12½, 14)"

LEFT
SLEEVE

2 (2, 3, 3)"

12 (15½, 16½, 18½)"

14 (17½, 19½, 21½)"

9"

Change to B and work 2 rows. Change to C and work until the piece measures 8½ (9, 10, 11½)" (21.5 [23, 25.5, 29]cm) from the beginning. Change to B and work 2 rows.

Bind off.

FRONT
Work as for the Back.

SLEEVES
Note Both Sleeves are worked the same until they split for the neck edge.

With smaller needle and A, cast on 36 stitches.

Work 1" (2.5cm) in garter stitch, ending with a wrong-side row.

Change to larger needles and stockinette stitch, increasing 1 stitch each edge every 4 (6, 4, 4) rows 6 (7, 12, 18) times—48 (50, 60, 72) stitches.

Extension for Front and Back Shoulders

Work until sleeve measures 12 (15½, 16½, 18½)" (30.5 [40.5, 42, 47]cm) from the beginning, ending with a wrong-side row.

Divide for Front and Back Neck

Right Sleeve

Next Row With right side facing, k24 (25, 30, 36) stitches, place

these stitches on a stitch holder for Front, join new ball of yarn and knit to end.

Back

Work on 24 (25, 30, 36) stitches only until the Right Sleeve measures 13½ (17, 19, 21)" (34.5 [43, 48.5, 53.5]cm), ending with a wrong-side row.

Change to B and work 2 rows. Change to C and work 2 rows. Bind off.

Front

With wrong side facing, slip stitches from the stitch holder. Join A and purl across. Work on 24 (25, 30, 36) stitches only until the Right Sleeve measures 13½ (17, 19, 21)" (34.5 [43, 48.5, 53.5]cm), ending with a wrong-side row. Slip stitches to a stitch holder for right center front ribbing.

Left Sleeve

Next Row With right side facing, k24 (25, 30, 36) stitches, place remaining stitches on a stitch holder for Front.

Back

Work on 24 (25, 30, 36) stitches only until the Left Sleeve measures 13½ (17, 19, 21)" (34.5 [43, 48.5, 53.5]cm), ending with a wrong-side row.

Change to B and work 2 rows.
Change to C and work 2 rows.
Bind off.

Front

With right side facing, slip stitches from the stitch holder. Join A and knit across. Work on 24 (25, 30, 36) stitches only until the Left Sleeve measures 13½ (17, 19, 21)" (34.5 [43, 48.5, 53.5]cm), ending with a wrong-side row. Slip stitches to a stitch holder for left center front rib.

HOOD

Sew the bound-off edge of the Back section of the Sleeves together to form the upper back of the sweater.

With right side facing and larger knitting needles, join A at the upper corner of front Right Sleeve, pick up and knit 8 (8, 12, 12) stitches along the edge of rows of the Right Sleeve (front neck), pick up and knit 16 (16, 24, 24) from the edge of rows along the Back neck, pick up and knit 8 (8, 12, 12) from edges of rows of left Front—32 (32, 48, 48) stitches.

Work in stockinette stitch until the Hood measures 8 (10, 11, 12)" (20.5 [25.5, 28, 30.5]cm) from the pick-up row, ending with a wrong-side row.

Decrease Row K14 (14, 22, 22), ssk, k2tog, knit to end.

Purl 1 row.

Repeat last 2 rows once more— 28 (28, 40, 40) stitches.

Bind off.

Fold bound-off row in half, and sew together to close the top of Hood.

Hood Ribbing

Slip stitches from right front center stitch holder to knitting needles. Join A and knit 24 (25, 30, 36) stitches, pick up and knit 95 (117, 129, 141) around the front edges of the Hood from left front center stitch holder—143 (167, 189, 213) stitches.

Change to B.
Row 1 (Wrong Side) P1, *k1, p1; repeat from * across.
Row 2 (Right Side) K1, *p1, k1; repeat from * across.

Change to C and repeat rows 1 and 2. Bind off in pattern.

FINISHING

Sew ribbing at center front closed for 2" (5cm).

Fit bound-off edges of Front and Back centered along edges of Sleeve/Hood section. Sew side and underarm seams. Weave in ends.

DOG SWEATER

Don't forget about the dog! How many times did I say that after Nora arrived? This warm cabled sweater is a special little reminder for the family pooch that you will still be a doting parent to them, too. Knit in a soft worsted-weight machine-washable wool, it works up quickly for your family's furry friend. After the baby's arrival, dress the pup in his or her special sweater, lace up your sneakers, put the baby in her buggy, and head off for a brisk walk to exercise the dog and walk off those extra baby pounds.

SKILL LEVEL
Intermediate

SIZES
One size, for small dog

FINISHED MEASUREMENTS
Chest: 15" (38cm)

Length: 16" (40.5cm)

YARN
3 balls of Mission Falls 1824 Wool, 100% superwash merino wool, 1¾ oz (50g), 84 yd (77m) in #011 Poppy, (4) medium

NEEDLES AND NOTIONS
- US size 6 (4mm) knitting needles
- US size 8 (5mm) knitting needles, or size needed to obtain gauge
- US size 6 (4mm) double-pointed knitting needles
- Cable needle
- Stitch holders
- Stitch marker
- Yarn needle

GAUGE
16 stitches and 24 rows = 4" (10cm) in stockinette stitch

Adjust needle size as necessary to obtain correct gauge.

ABBREVIATIONS
C4F: Slip next 2 stitches to a cable needle and hold in front. Knit the next 2 stitches from the left-hand needle. Knit the stitches from the cable needle.

K1f&b: This is an easy increase stitch. Knit into the next stitch, but before removing it from the left-hand needle, knit again into the back loop of the same stitch. Remove the stitch from the left-hand needle—1 stitch increased.

BACK
With smaller needles, cast on 42 stitches.

Row 1 (Wrong Side) P2, *k2, p2; repeat from * across.
Row 2 (Right Side) K2, *p2, k2; repeat from * across.

Repeat the last 2 rows until the piece measures 2½" (6.5cm) from the beginning, ending with

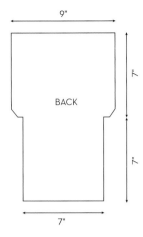

9"

BACK

7"

7"

7"

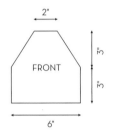

2"

FRONT

3"

3"

6"

CABLE PATTERN

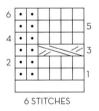

6 STITCHES

STITCH KEY

☐ = K on right side,
p on wrong side

▣ = P on right side,
k on wrong side

▨ = Slip 2 stitches onto
cable needle and hold
in front, k2, k2 from
cable needle

a wrong-side row. Change to larger needles.

Row 1 (Right Side) K2, p2, repeat Row 1 of Chart to last 2 stitches, k2.

Row 2 P2, k2, repeat Row 2 of Chart to last 2 stitches, p2.

Row 3 K2, p2, repeat Row 3 of Chart to last 2 stitches, k2.

Row 4 P2, k2, repeat Row 4 of Chart to last 2 stitches, p2.

Row 5 K2, p2, repeat Row 5 of Chart to last 2 stitches, k2.

Row 6 P2, k2, repeat Row 6 of Chart to last 2 stitches, p2.

Repeat rows 1–6 until the piece measures 7" (18cm) from the beginning, ending with a wrong-side row.

Shape Shoulders

Cast on 2 stitches at the beginning of the next 2 rows.

Continuing to work in Cable Pattern as established and working the new stitches in stockinette stitch, work 2 more rows.

Increase Row K2, k1f&b, continue in established pattern to last 3 stitches, k1f&b, k2.

Continue in pattern, working new stitches in reverse stockinette stitch and repeating Increase Row on next right side row once—50 stitches.

Continue in pattern, working until the piece measures 14" (35.5cm) from the beginning, ending with a wrong-side row. Slip stitches to a stitch holder.

FRONT

With larger needles, cast on 30 stitches. Work in stockinette stitch until the piece measures 3" (7.5cm) from the beginning, ending with a wrong-side row.

Increase Row K1, ssk, knit to last 3 stitches, k2tog, k1.

Purl 1 row.

Repeat the last 2 rows 10 times—10 stitches.

Slip stitches on a stitch holder.

FINISHING

Lining up stitches on stitch holders for collar, sew Front and Back together along straight edges, leaving 2½" (6.5cm) open for the leg holes. Adjust the placement of the leg holes to fit your dog.

Collar

With right side facing, slip the Back and Front stitches from the stitch holders to double-pointed knitting needles.

Row 1 *K2, p2; repeat from * across the Back stitches, repeat from * across the Front stitches—60 stitches. Divide evenly among needles. Join to work in the round, being careful not to twist the stitches; place a marker for the beginning of the round.

Continue in ribbing until the collar measures 2" (5cm). Bind off loosely.

Weave in ends. Lightly block.

What About the Dog?

"WHAT ABOUT THE DOG?" WAS A QUESTION I OFTEN ASKED. With the arrival of our second child, it was just more difficult to go for a good long walk on the dog's schedule. The baby's schedule trumped all of ours. Zuzu, our Boston terrier, looked sad and confused. What was this crying baby? Why did he get to sleep on the bed when she couldn't? What had taken over her favorite lap? Zuzu adjusted to the new arrival, and by the time Cole was nine months old, he and Zuzu were best friends. Before your baby arrives, here are some basic steps that you should take to prepare your dog or cat.

1. Update all your pet's vaccines and shots.

2. During the pregnancy, Mom should not clean or empty the litter box. Let Dad do that chore for the next nine months.

3. Invest in some obedience training. You want the dog to obey the basic commands of sit, stay, and come.

4. Ask a friend to tape her baby for a few hours. Play these sounds to help your pet become accustomed to infant sounds.

5. Schedule someone to watch the family pets while you're in the hospital.

6. When the baby arrives home, let Daddy carry the baby into the house so Mom can greet the family pets.

7. Invest in a screen for the door of the baby's room so pets can't enter the room when the baby is sleeping.

8. Knit a soft sweater that your dog can wear for cold weather walks.

ZUZU THE DOG

A dog is a boy's best friend. Our Boston terrier, Zuzu, is definitely Cole's best friend. Zuzu crawls, eats off the floor, and hides under the couch—all the things that Cole wants to do. Knit in black, white, and red washable wools, this pliable knitted dog is a perfect first toy. The high-contrast colors will surely capture your baby's attention.

SKILL LEVEL
Intermediate

FINISHED MEASUREMENTS
5" (12.5cm) tall by 7" (18cm) long

YARN
1 skein each of Karabella Yarns Aurora 8, 100% superfine merino wool, 1¾ oz (50g), 98 yd (89m) in #1148 Black (A), #1350 White (B), and #5 Red (C), (4) medium

NEEDLES AND NOTIONS
- US size 4 (3.5mm) knitting needles, or size needed to obtain gauge
- Stitch holders
- Bobbins
- Yarn needle
- Polyester fiber filling
- Scraps of yarn for face embroidery

GAUGE
22 stitches and 36 rows = 4" (10cm) in stockinette stitch

Adjust needle size as necessary to obtain correct gauge.

NOTES:
1. The spots on Zuzu are worked in intarsia, using a different ball of yarn for each color change. Wind bobbins for each color.
2. Pick up the new color from under the old color to twist the yarns and prevent holes.
3. Short rows are used to shape the nose.

ABBREVIATIONS
K1f&b: This is an easy increase stitch. Knit into the next stitch, but before removing it from the left-hand needle, knit again into the back loop of the same stitch. Remove the stitch from the left-hand needle—1 stitch increased.

SHORT ROWS
Wrap and turn: Bring yarn to front, slip next stitch, turn, wrap yarn around slip stitch and slip same stitch back onto the right-hand needle. On the next row, work wrapped stitch by picking up wrap and working together with the stitch on the left-hand needle.

LEFT SIDE

Front Leg

With A, cast on 5 stitches.

Row 1 Purl.
Row 2 K1f&b, k3, k1f&b—
7 stitches.
Row 3 Purl.
Row 4 Knit.
Row 5 Purl.
Row 6 K1f&b, k5, k1f&b—
9 stitches.
Row 7 Purl.

Cut yarn, leaving a 4" (10cm) tail.
Slip stitches to a stitch holder.

Back Leg

With A, cast on 5 stitches.

Row 1 Purl.
Row 2 K1f&b, k3, k1f&b—
7 stitches.
Row 3 Purl.
Row 4 Knit.
Row 5 Purl.
Row 6 K1f&b, k5, k1f&b—
9 stitches.
Row 7 Purl.

Join for Body

Row 8 Knit 9 stitches, cast on
9 stitches, knit 9 stitches from
Front Leg stitch holder—27
stitches.
Row 9 Purl.
Row 10 K1f&b, knit to last stitch,
k1f&b—29 stitches.
Row 11 Purl.

Row 12 K1f&b, knit to last stitch,
k1f&b—31 stitches.
Row 13 Purl.
Row 14 K1f&b, knit to last stitch,
k1f&b—33 stitches.
Row 15 Purl.
Row 16 K1, ssk, knit across—
32 stitches.
Row 17 Purl.
Row 18 K1, ssk, knit across—
31 stitches.
Row 19 Purl.
Row 20 K1, ssk, knit across—
30 stitches.
Row 21 Purl.
Row 22 Knit.
Row 23 Purl.
Row 24 Knit.

Bind off. The edge with less
shaping is the neck edge.

RIGHT SIDE

Back Leg

With A, cast on 5 stitches.

Row 1 Purl.
Row 2 K1f&b, k3, k1f&b—
7 stitches.
Row 3 Purl.
Row 4 Knit.
Row 5 Purl.
Row 6 K1f&b, k5, k1f&b—
9 stitches.
Row 7 Purl.

Cut yarn, leaving a 4" (10cm) tail.
Slip stitches to a stitch holder.

Front Leg

With A, cast on 5 stitches.

Row 1 Purl.
Row 2 K1f&b, k3, k1f&b—7 stitches.
Row 3 Purl.
Row 4 Knit.
Row 5 Purl.
Row 6 K1f&b, k5, k1f&b—9 stitches.
Row 7 Purl.

Join for Body

Row 8 K9 stitches, cast on 9 stitches, knit 9 stitches from Back Leg stitch holder—27 stitches.
Row 9 Purl.
Row 10 K1f&b, knit to last stitch, k1f&b—29 stitches.
Row 11 Purl.
Row 12 K1f&b, knit to last stitch, k1f&b—31 stitches.
Row 13 Purl
Row 14 K1f&b, knit to last stitch, k1f&b—33 stitches.
Row 15 Purl.
Row 16 Knit to last 3 stitches, k2tog, k1—32 stitches.
Row 17 Purl.
Row 18 Knit to last 3 stitches, k2tog, k1—31 stitches.
Row 19 Purl.
Row 20 Knit to last 3 stitches, k2tog, k1—30 stitches.
Row 21 Purl.
Row 22 Knit.

Row 23 Purl.
Row 24 Knit.

Bind off. The edge with less shaping is the neck edge.

BELLY

With B, cast on 3 stitches.

Row 1 Purl.
Row 2 K1f&b, k1, k1f&b—5 stitches.
Row 3 Purl.
Row 4 Knit.
Row 5 Purl.
Row 6 K1f&b, knit to last stitch, k1f&b—7 stitches.
Row 7 Purl.
Row 8 Knit.
Row 9 Purl.
Row 10 K1f&b, knit to last stitch, k1f&b—9 stitches.
Row 11 Purl.
Row 12 Knit.
Row 13 Purl.
Row 14 Cast on 8 stitches, knit across—17 stitches.
Row 15 Cast on 8 stitches, purl across—25 stitches.
Row 16 Knit.
Row 17 Purl.
Row 18 Knit.
Row 19 Purl.
Row 20 Knit.
Row 21 Purl.
Row 22 Bind off 7 stitches, knit to end—18 stitches.
Row 23 Bind off 7 stitches, purl to end—11 stitches.

Row 24 K7 with B, knit 4 with A.

Row 25 P4 with A, purl 7 with B.

Row 26 K6 with B, knit 5 with A.

Row 27 P5 with A , purl 6 with B.

Row 28 K9 with B, knit 2 with A.

Row 29 P2 with A, purl 9 with B.

Row 30 K8 with B, knit 3 with A.

Row 31 P3 with A, purl 8 with B.

Row 32 Cast on 8 stitches with B, knit 8 with B, knit 3 with A—19 stitches.

Row 33 Cast on 8 stitches with A, knit 3 with A, knit 16 with B—27 stitches.

Row 34 K14 with B, knit 13 with A.

Row 35 P13 with A, purl 14 with B.

Row 36 K15 with B, knit 12 with A.

Row 37 P12 with A, purl 15 with B.

Row 38 K15 with B, knit 12 with A.

Row 39 P12 with A, knit 15 with B.

Row 40 Bind off 8 stitches, knit 7 with B, knit 12 with A.

Row 41 Bind off 8 stitches, purl 4 with A, purl 7 with B—11 stitches.

Row 42 K1, ssk, knit 4 with B, k1, k2tog, k1 with A—9 stitches.

Row 43 P3 with A, purl 6 with B.

Row 44 K1, ssk, knit 3 stitches with B, k2tog, k1 with A—7 stitches.

Row 45 P2 with A, purl 5 with B.

Row 46 With B, k1, ssk, k1, k2tog, k1—5 stitches.

Row 47 Purl with B.

Row 48 With B, k1, slip 1 stitch, k2tog, pass slipped stitch over, k1—3 stitches.

Row 49 Purl.

Bind off. The bound-off edge is the neck edge.

NECK

Sew the 2 sides together along the straight, back edge, leaving the last 1½" (4cm) unsewn for neck.

With right side facing and C, pick up and knit 14 stitches at neck.

Knit for 4 rows. Bind off.

FRONT OF HEAD

Row 1 With A, cast on 5 stitches.

Row 2 Purl.

Row 3 K1f&b, knit to last stitch, k1f&b—7 stitches.

Row 4 Purl.

Row 5 K1f&b, knit to last stitch, k1f&b—9 stitches.

Row 6 Purl.

Row 7 K1f&b, knit to last stitch, k1f&b—11 stitches.

Row 8 Purl.

NOSE

Row 9 K7, wrap and turn.
P3, wrap and turn.
K4, wrap and turn.
P5, wrap and turn.
K6, wrap and turn.
P7, wrap and turn.
K9, wrap and turn.
Purl to end—11 stitches.

Row 10 K3 with A, knit 8 with B.

Row 11 P8 with B, purl 3 with A.

Row 12 With A, k1, k2tog, k2, with B, k3, k2tog, k1—9 stitches.
Row 13 P5 with B, purl 4 with A.
Row 14 With A, k1, k2tog, k2, with B, k1, k2tog, k1—7 stitches.
Row 15 P3 with B, purl 4 with A.
Row 16 With A, k1, k2tog, k1, with B, k2tog, k1—5 stitches.

Bind off.

BACK OF HEAD

Row 1 With A, cast on 5 stitches.
Row 2 Purl.
Row 3 K1f&b, knit to last stitch, k1f&b—7 stitches.
Row 4 Purl.
Row 5 K1f&b, knit to last stitch, k1f&b—9 stitches.
Row 6 Purl.
Row 7 K1f&b, knit to last stitch, k1f&b—11 stitches.
Rows 8-18 Work in stockinette stitch.
Row 19 K1, k2tog, knit to last 3 stitches, k2tog, k1—9 stitches.
Row 20 Purl.
Row 21 K1, k2tog, knit to last 3 stitches, k2tog, k1—7 stitches.
Row 22 Purl.
Row 23 K1, k2tog, k1, k2tog, k1—5 stitches.

Bind off.

EARS (MAKE 2)

With A, cast on 7 stitches.

Row 1 Purl.
Row 2 K1, ssk, k1, k2tog, k1—5 stitches.
Row 3 Purl.
Row 4 Knit.
Row 5 Purl.
Row 6 K1, slip 1 stitch, k2tog, pass slipped stitch over, k1—3 stitches.
Row 7 Purl.
Row 8 Slip 1 stitch, k2tog, pass slipped stitch over. Fasten off.

TAIL

With A, cast on 5 stitches.
Bind off.

FINISHING

Fit Belly into sewn Body pieces and sew together, leaving a small opening for stuffing. Stuff Body, and sew opening closed. Sew Head pieces together, leaving the neck edge open for stuffing. Stuff Head, and sew to the neck edge of Body. Sew cast-on edge of each Ear onto Head. Sew Tail to Body.

Using scraps of yarn, embroider the eyes and nose onto the Head. Weave in ends.

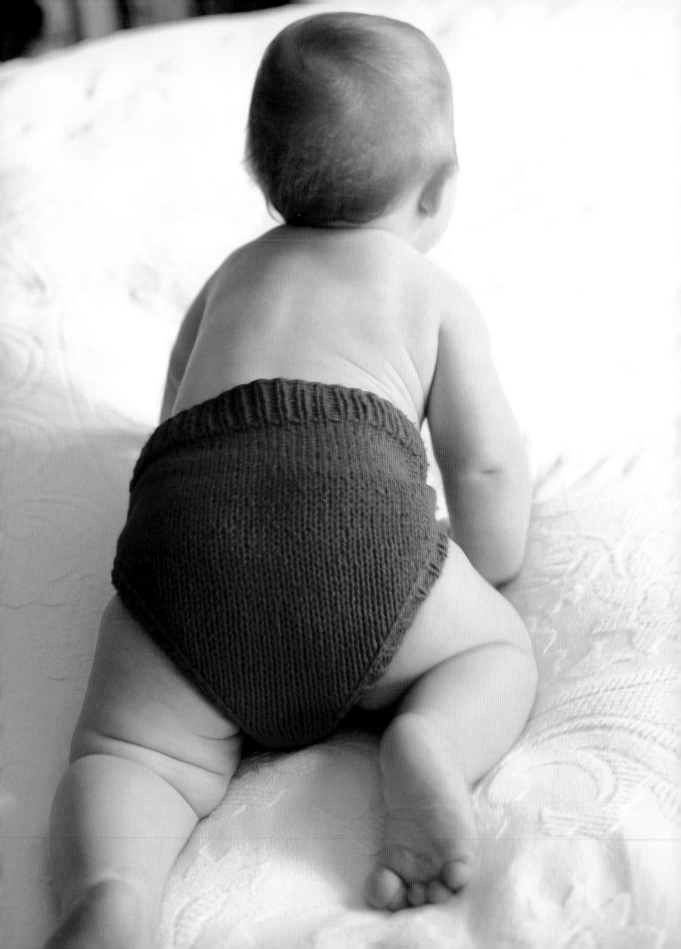

DIAPER COVERS

So many diaper options. Whatever you choose, a fashionable diaper cover is essential. Because knitting a diaper cover is as easy as knitting a hat, you can knit up one for every day of the week. Select yarns and fibers to coordinate with your baby's wardrobe. The diaper covers have an old-fashioned look, but knit in bright colors, they will be ultra-fashionable.

SKILL LEVEL

Intermediate

SIZES

0–6 months (12 months, 18 months, 24 months)

FINISHED MEASUREMENTS

Waist: 16 (17½, 18½, 20½)" (41 [44.5, 47, 52]cm)

YARN

1 skein of O-Wool Classic, 100% certified organic merino wool, 3½ oz (100g), 198 yd (181m) in #4400 Sumac, #2300 Sky, #4202 Thistle, #4302 Willow, or #6402 Saffron, (4) medium

NEEDLES AND NOTIONS

- US size 4 (3.5mm) double-pointed knitting needles
- US size 6 (4mm) double-pointed knitting needles, or size needed to obtain gauge
- Stitch markers
- Stitch holders
- Yarn needle

GAUGE

18 stitches and 28 rows = 4" (10cm) in stockinette stitch using larger needles

Adjust needle size as necessary to obtain correct gauge.

NOTES

1. Diaper covers are knit in the round from the waist down.
2. Short rows are used to add fullness to the Back.

ABBREVIATIONS

K2tog: (An easy right-slanting decrease.) Knit the next 2 stitches together through the front loops at the same time.

Ssk: (A slightly more advanced decrease that slants left. Worked with the K2tog, it will produce a mirrored decrease that will make your garments look very professional.) Slip the next 2 stitches individually

from the left-hand needle to the right-hand needle as if to knit. Then place the left-hand needle into these 2 stitches through the front loops and, using your right-hand needle, which is now in the back loops of these stitches, knit them together.

M1R: Find the horizontal bar between the last completed

stitch on the right-hand needle and the next stitch on the left-hand needle. Using the left-hand needle, pick up the horizontal bar by inserting the left-hand needle from front to back. Knit the raised bar through the back loop. (**Hint:** If you have a hole, you may have knit the raised bar through the front loop.)

M1L: Find the horizontal bar between the last completed stitch on the right-hand needle and the next stitch on the left-hand needle. Using the left-hand needle, pick up the horizontal bar by inserting the left-hand needle from back to front. Knit the raised bar through the front loop. (**Hint:** If you have a hole, you may have knit the raised bar through the back loop.)

SHORT ROWS

Wrap and turn: Bring yarn to front, slip next stitch, turn, wrap yarn around slipped stitch, and slip same stitch back onto the right-hand needle. On the next round, work wrapped stitch by picking up wrap and working together with the stitch on the left-hand needle.

DIAPER COVER

Cast on 72 (80, 84, 92) stitches using the smaller needle. Join to work in the round being careful not to twist stitches; place marker for beginning of round.

Round 1 *K1, p1; repeat from * around for waist ribbing. Repeat Round 1 until rib measures 1¼" (3cm).

Next Round Change to larger needles, k36 (40, 42, 46), place marker, knit around.

Back Shaping (Short Rows)
K23 (25, 26, 28) stitches, wrap and turn.
P10 stitches, wrap and turn.
K14 (14, 16, 16) stitches, wrap and turn.
P18 (18, 22, 22) stitches, wrap and turn.
K22 (22, 26, 26) stitches, wrap and turn.
P26 (26, 30, 30) stitches, wrap and turn.
K30 (30, 34, 34) stitches, wrap and turn.
P34 (34, 37, 37) stitches, wrap and turn.

Mark this last round for measuring later.

Work all stitches in stockinette stitch in the round until the garment measures 2 (2½, 3, 3)" (5 [6.5, 7.5, 7.5]cm) from the locking marker. Note that the back of the soaker will be longer than the front due to the short row shaping.

4,000 Diapers

IN OUR HOUSE, CHORES ARE DIVIDED FAIRLY: Alan is in charge of trash and sanitation, I handle laundry, and we share food preparation. So, diapers fell clearly under Alan's responsibility. And he was worried about them! What about a Diaper Genie? Alan sadly learned that the Genie did not magically dispose of diapers. How many will we use hourly, daily, weekly, monthly—annually? Where will all those dirty diapers go? Should we consider other options? I think he considered cloth diapers only so that disposal issues turned into laundry issues—my chore.

You can expect to change between 4,000 and 5,000 diapers over baby's first three years. Disposables have to go somewhere. Approximately 18 billion disposable diapers end up in U.S. landfills each year (calculations by Donella H. Meadows, adjunct professor of environmental studies at Dartmouth College). Cloth diapers, on the other hand, can be costly and put a strain on water resources. Here are a couple of websites to visit as you explore your diapering options: www.realdiaperassociation.org/diaperfacts.php and www.parentingbynature.com/cloth_diapers_top_10.php

If you choose cloth diapers, there is a costly initial investment, but at least you won't have to run to the grocery store at 11 pm because you just ran out of diapers. For newborns, you need about 10 diapers per day, so purchase at least three days' worth of diapers. You'll also need about 5–7 diaper covers.

The Diaper Covers on page 108 are an excellent choice. Wool can absorb up to one-third of its weight in moisture. Wool also is antibacterial, so if the covers get wet, just let them air dry. I recommend washing your soakers weekly. Re-lanolize them if they start to leak. Simply fill the sink with cold water and dissolve 1 teaspoon of pure lanolin (if you breastfeed, you can use the same lanolin cream that you use to soothe cracked nipples) in the water. Soak the Diaper Covers, inside out, for 15 minutes, then air dry.

Shape Hips

Increase Round Slip marker, *k1, M1R, knit to 1 stitch before next marker, M1L, k1, slip marker; repeat from * around—76 (84, 88, 96) stitches; 4 stitches increased.

Work 3 (4, 5, 5) rounds even.

Repeat the last 4 (5, 6, 6) rounds 2 (2, 2, 1) more times—84 (92, 96, 100) stitches.

Divide for Leg Openings

Back

Knit to marker and turn.

Purl to marker and slip unworked 42 (46, 48, 50) stitches to a stitch holder.

Decrease Row With right side facing, k1, ssk, knit to last 3 stitches, k2tog, k1.

Continue to decrease every right-side row until 12 (14, 12, 14) stitches remain. Place remaining stitches on a stitch holder.

Front

With right side facing, knit the 42 (46, 48, 50) stitches from the holder and turn.

Purl 1 row.

Decrease Row With right side facing, k1, ssk, knit to last 3 stitches, k2tog, k1.

Continue to decrease every right-side row until 12 (14, 12, 14)

stitches remain. Cut yarn, leaving approximately 6" (15cm) for grafting.

Grafting Front and Back Stitches

Slip remaining stitches of the Front and Back to separate larger needles. Hold needles with wrong sides facing each other.

1. Thread yarn needle with yarn.
2. Set up stitches; put the yarn needle into the first stitch on the front knitting needle as if to purl, and pull the yarn through. Next, pull the yarn needle through the first stitch on the rear knitting needle as if to knit.
3. Pull the yarn needle through the first stitch on the front knitting needle again as if to knit and slip the stitch off the knitting needle. Next, pull the yarn needle through the second stitch on the front knitting needle as if to purl, but leave this stitch on the knitting needle.
4. Pull the yarn needle through the first stitch on the rear knitting needle as if to purl and slip the stitch off the knitting needle. Next, pull the yarn needle through the second stitch on the rear knitting needle as if to knit.

Repeat Steps 3 and 4 to the end of the row.

Leg Edgings

Using smaller double-pointed knitting needles, pick up and knit 40 (44, 46, 50) stitches around one leg opening. Divide stitches evenly among needles. Join stitches to work in the round, being careful not to twist stitches; place marker for beginning of round.

Round 1 *K1, p1; repeat from * around for ribbing.

Repeat Round 1 until ribbing measures 1¼" (3cm).

Bind off loosely.

Repeat for second leg opening.

FINISHING

Weave in ends. Lightly block.

LEG WARMERS

Crawling. Climbing. Running. Once babies get the hang of crawling, they are always on the move. These leg warmers, which will protect pudgy knees as your baby starts to explore, are a snap to knit—and they even make 2 a.m. diaper changes easier. Big sister may even steal them for arm warmers when she sees the rainbow of colors. With the extra yarn, knit a second pair just for her!

SKILL LEVEL
Easy

SIZES
0–6 months (12 months, 18–24 months)

FINISHED MEASUREMENTS
Ankle Circumference: 5 (6, 7)" (12.5 [15, 18]cm)

Upper Leg Circumference: 6½ (7½, 8½)" (16.5 [19, 21.5]cm)

Length: 10 (12, 15)" (25.5 [30.5, 38]cm)

YARN
1 ball each of Karabella Yarns Aurora 4, 100% super fine merino wool, 1¾ oz (50g), 197 yd (180m) in #11 Red (A), #4 Tangerine (B), #8171 Yellow (C), #16 Jade (D), #22 Periwinkle (E), and #17 Royal (F), (🔢) super fine

NEEDLES AND NOTIONS
- US size 2 (2.75mm) double-pointed knitting needles, or size needed to obtain gauge
- Stitch markers
- Yarn needle

GAUGE
28 stitches and 32 rows = 4" (20cm) in stockinette stitch

Adjust needle size as necessary to obtain correct gauge.

NOTE
The Leg Warmers are knit in the round from the ankle up.

ABBREVIATIONS
M1R: Find the horizontal bar between the last completed stitch on the right-hand needle and the next stitch on the left-hand needle. Using the left-hand needle, pick up the horizontal bar by inserting the left-hand needle from front to back. Knit the raised bar through the back loop. (**Hint:** If you have a hole, you may have knit the raised bar through the front loop)

M1L: Find the horizontal bar between the last completed stitch on the right-hand needle and the next stitch on the left-hand needle. Using the left-hand needle, pick up the horizontal bar by inserting the left-hand needle from back to front. Knit the raised bar through the front loop. (**Hint:** If you have a hole, you may have knit the raised bar through the back loop.)

LEG WARMERS

With A, cast on 36 (42, 50) stitches. Join to work in the round, being careful not to twist the stitches; place a marker for the beginning of the round.

Round 1 *K1, p1; repeat from * for ribbing.

Repeat round 1 for a total of 7 (10, 12) rounds.

Change to B and stockinette stitch and knit 8 (9, 12) rounds.

Change to C and knit 8 (9, 12) rounds.

Change to D and knit 5 (6, 9) rounds.
Increase Round K1, M1R, knit to last stitch, M1L, k1—38 (44, 52) stitches.
Knit 2 rounds.

Change to E and knit 8 (9, 12) rounds.

Change to F and knit 3 (4, 7) rounds.
Repeat Increase Round—40 (46, 54) stitches.
Knit 4 rounds.

Change to A and knit 7 (8, 11) rounds.
Repeat Increase Round—42 (48, 56) stitches.

Change to B and knit 8 (9, 12) rounds.

Change to C and knit 6 (7, 10) rounds.
Repeat Increase Round—44 (50, 58) stitches.
Knit 1 round.

Change D and knit 8 (9, 12) rounds.
Change to E and knit 4 (5, 8) rounds.
Repeat Increase Round—46 (52, 60) stitches.
Knit 3 rounds.

Change to F and knit 8 (9, 12) rounds.

Change to A and knit 1 round.
Next Round *K1, p1; repeat from *.
Continue in ribbing for 6 (9, 11) more rounds.

Bind off.

FINISHING

Weave in ends. Lightly block.

SHAWL SWEATER

During your pregnancy, don't forget to pamper yourself! Surround yourself with luxury. This item is perfect to pack in your hospital bag. It will ward off the hospital chills as well as swathe a nursing baby. Knit in the softest hand-painted cashmere, this wrap is a dream to knit. Its luxurious nature means that you'll delight in it long after the baby is out of diapers.

SKILL LEVEL
Beginner

SIZE
One size fits most.

FINISHED MEASUREMENTS
20" (51cm) wide by 65" (165cm) long

YARN
4 skeins of Artyarns Cashmere 2, 100% 2-stranded cashmere, 1¾ oz (50g), 255 yd (233m) in #CS137 Tan/Beige, (3) light

NEEDLES AND NOTIONS
- US size 9 (6mm) circular knitting needle, long enough to accommodate stitches, or size needed to obtain gauge
- US size H-8 (5mm) crochet hook
- Yarn needle

GAUGE
24 stitches and 26 rows = 4" (20cm) in Rib Pattern

Adjust needle size as necessary to obtain correct gauge.

NOTES
1. The Shawl Sweater is knit back and forth in rows on a circular needle to accommodate the large number of stitches.
2. Every pregnant belly is unique, and this shawl is easy to size up or down. To enlarge it, add a few inches (centimeters) between the armholes. To shrink it, take away a few inches (centimeters). Just remember, if you make it larger, you may need more yarn.

E-LOOP CAST-ON METHOD
Wrap the yarn around the outside of your left thumb and insert your needle into the wrapped loop as if to knit. Transfer this loop from your thumb to the right-hand needle.

RIB PATTERN
Row 1 K4, *p2, k4; repeat from * to end.

Row 2 P4, *k2, p4; repeat from * to end.

SHAWL SWEATER
Cast on 124 stitches. Work in Rib Pattern until the piece measures 22½" (57cm) from the beginning, ending with a wrong-side row.

Shape Armhole

Bind-Off Row With right side facing, work in Rib Pattern for 30 stitches, bind off 48 stitches, work across.

Cast-On Row Work in Rib Pattern for 46 stitches, cast on 48 stitches over bound-off stitches of previous row, work in pattern to end.

Continue in Rib Pattern until the piece measures 20" (51cm) from the armhole.

Shape Second Armhole

Bind-Off Row With right side facing, work in Rib Pattern for 30 stitches, bind off 48 stitches, work across.

Cast-On Row Work in Rib Pattern for 46 stitches, cast on 48 stitches over bound-off stitches of previous row, work in pattern to end.

Continue in Rib Pattern until the piece measures 65" (165cm) from the beginning. Bind off stitches in pattern.

FINISHING

Edging

With right side facing and crochet hook, join yarn at lower armhole. Single crochet evenly around the armhole; slip stitch to first stitch to join. Repeat on second armhole.

Weave in ends. Block the entire piece lightly to soften the Rib Pattern.

The Final Stretch

THE LAST THREE MONTHS OF YOUR PREGNANCY can feel like the longest three months of your life. Conversely, the first three months of your baby's life will be the shortest. It's just not fair. By the end of the next three months, you'll tire of telling people your due date. A good night's sleep may be difficult. Shoes may not fit. And worst of all, you can develop a pregnancy-related form of carpal tunnel syndrome. During my first pregnancy, because of mild swelling and carpal tunnel syndrome, I found it difficult to knit. While I carried Cole, I took care to massage my hands and wrists, elevate my hands at night, and drink lots of water to prevent this syndrome. Be sure to mention any pain and excessive swelling to your doctor. Edema is a normal part of pregnancy, but excessive swelling can be an early indicator of preeclampsia.

This chapter offers tips and knitting projects to help you through the final months. Most of these projects are simply made with garter or stockinette stitch. These smaller projects—cotton wash cloths, socks, hats, and a bib— are quick, easy knits and perfect distractions as you near the big day.

Third Trimester

Week 28: Baby is now about 2 pounds. She will gain about another 5–7 pounds in the coming weeks as she prepares for her birthday.

Week 29: The time is right to develop your birth plan.

Week 30: Consider preregistering at the hospital. It will save time when baby decides the time to come is 4 a.m.

Week 31: Is the nursery ready? Get the necessary gear and knit your Baby Essentials Kit (opposite page).

Week 32: Sing to your baby. How about Doozer's Knitting Song from Fraggle Rock? Here are just a few lines: "It's neat and it's sweet.
It's a ding dong treat,
knittin' socks for little feet.
Just sittin' with your knittin' all day long."

Week 33: Swollen feet? Kick off the shoes, grab a knitting project, and relax with your feet up.

Week 34: Talk with your other children—and pets—about the baby's arrival. Show off the beautiful sweaters that you've made for them.

Week 35: Bouncing baby? Your baby may be having her first bout of hiccups.

Week 36: Feeling bloated? Mild swelling is a natural part of pregnancy. Call your doctor is you have severe or sudden bloating, as it may be an indicator of preeclampsia.

Week 37: Pack your bags. Be sure to include your cashmere Shawl Sweater, the Take-Me-Home Swaddle Blanket, and your favorite knitted garment.

Week 38: At your weekly doctor's appointment, the doctor will probably check to see if you have dilated—a good sign that the baby will be on her way soon. Ask again who to call when you go into labor.

Week 39: Support is essential. The time is right to shop for a good nursing bra.

Week 40: Your water broke! Don't worry if it happens at the bus stop, while shopping at the mall, or at bedtime. Call your doctor, and head to the hospital.

BABY ESSENTIALS KIT

This washable cotton case, filled with a baby's comb, clippers, thermometer, and scissors, is a must-have. Rolled up, it fits perfectly between the diapers and bottles in any fashionable diaper bag.

SKILL LEVEL
Beginner

FINISHED MEASUREMENTS
12" (30.5cm) wide by 8" (20.5cm) long

YARN
1 skein of Blue Sky Alpacas Dyed Cotton, 100% organically grown cotton, 3½ oz (100g), 150 yd (137m) in #5631 Circus Peanut, (4) medium

NEEDLES AND NOTIONS
- US size 8 (5mm) knitting needles, or size needed to obtain gauge
- Yarn needle
- 1 yd (1m) twill ribbon, 9/16" (14mm) wide
- Sewing needle and matching thread

GAUGE
16 stitches and 20 rows = 4" (10cm) in stockinette stitch

Adjust needle size as necessary to obtain correct gauge.

ESSENTIALS KIT
Cast on 50 stitches. Work in stockinette stitch until the piece measures 4" (10cm) from the beginning, ending with a right-side row.

Knit 1 row on the wrong side for turning row.

Continue in stockinette stitch until the piece measures 12" (30.5cm) from the beginning. Bind off.

FINISHING
With wrong sides together, fold the 4" (10cm) section along the turning row. Sew right-side edge closed. Cut two lengths of ribbon, each 15" (38cm) long. Insert one end of each ribbon piece in the left side seam and sew side closed, catching ribbon ends securely. Divide pocket made into 3 sections, each 2" (5cm) wide, and 2 sections, each 3" (7.5cm). With sewing needle and thread, sew through both layers of pocket to sew sections closed. These sections will form pockets to carry all your essentials.

Weave in ends. Lightly block.

WASH CLOTHS

There is nothing sweeter than the smell of a freshly bathed baby. Bath time can be a quiet time just before getting ready for bed. Knit in the supplest cotton, these hand-crafted wash cloths only accentuate one of the most intimate moments between baby and parent. I bet you'll knit a few for yourself, too.

SKILL LEVEL
Beginner

FINISHED MEASUREMENTS
10" (25.5cm) wide by 8" (20.5cm) long

YARN
1 skein each of Blue Sky Alpacas Organic Cotton, 100% organic cotton, 3½ oz (100g), 150 yd (137m) in #80 Bone (A) and #85 Willow (C), (4) medium

1 skein each of Blue Sky Alpacas Dyed Cotton, 100% organically grown cotton, 3½ oz (100g), 150 yd (137m) in #606 Shell (B) and #616 Sky (D), (4) medium

NEEDLES AND NOTIONS
- US size 8 (5mm) knitting needles, or size needed to obtain gauge
- Yarn needle

GAUGE
16 stitches and 20 rows = 4" (10cm) in stockinette stitch

Adjust needle size as necessary to obtain correct gauge.

VERSION 1
With A or B, cast on 39 stitches.

Row 1 *K3, p3; repeat from * across, end k3.
Repeat row 1 until the piece measures 8" (20.5cm) from the beginning. Bind off.

VERSION 2
With C or D, cast on 39 stitches.

Knit every row until the piece measures 8" (20.5cm) from the beginning. Bind off.

FINISHING
Weave in ends.

BABY BIB

Baby's breath smells so sweet, but spittle is another story. The Baby Bib is a super-quick knit, so make a few extras to catch the unavoidable spit-up.

SKILL LEVEL
Beginner

FINISHED MEASUREMENTS
7" (18 cm) wide by 7½" (19cm) long

YARN
1 skein of Blue Sky Alpacas Organic Cotton, 100% organic cotton, 3½ oz (100g), 150 yd (137m) in #80 Bone, medium

NEEDLES AND NOTIONS
- US size 8 (5mm) knitting needles, or size needed to obtain gauge
- US size 8 (5mm) double-pointed knitting needles
- Stitch holders
- Yarn needle

GAUGE
16 stitches and 20 rows = 4" (10cm) in stockinette stitch

Adjust needle size as necessary to obtain correct gauge.

BIB
Cast on 20 stitches.

Knit 2 rows.

Next Row (Right Side) K2, M1, knit to last 2 stitches, M1, k2.

Next Row K2, purl to last 2 stitches, k2.

Repeat the last 2 rows until 28 stitches.

Continue working in stockinette stitch, keeping first and last 2 stitches in garter stitch, until the piece measures 5" (12.5cm) from the beginning, ending with a wrong-side row.

Next Row (Right Side) K2, ssk, knit to last 4 stitches, k2tog, k2.
Next Row K2, purl to last 2 stitches, k2.

Repeat the last 2 rows until 22 stitches remain. Place these stitches on a stitch holder.

TIE
With double-pointed needle, cast on 4 stitches. Work stockinette stitch until the Tie measures 12" (30.5cm) from the beginning.

EDGING
Slip the Bib stitches from a stitch holder onto an extra needle.

1. Knit 4 stitches from the Tie.
2. Slip these 4 stitches onto the beginning of the extra needle holding the Bib stitches.

3. Knit 5 stitches.
4. Bind off the last knit stitch.
5. Slip these 4 stitches from the right-hand needle back to the left-hand needle.

Repeat steps 3-5 until the Bib stitches are completely bound off.

Continue working the remaining 4 stitches of the Tie in stockinette stitch for 12" (30.5cm) more. Bind off.

FINISHING
Weave in ends.

Planning the Nursery

WITH ONLY WEEKS TO GO, PREPARATIONS SHOULD BE IN FULL FORCE. So let's get to work on the nursery and the essential baby gear. Pick up any baby magazine and discover the 500 items that they believe you will desperately need. We live in a Victorian row house with limited storage space. Everything that enters the house must be necessary (except yarn, of course!). This is the philosophy I used when selecting gear for Nora and Cole. My essentials list included

- Car seat
- Stroller (preferably one that converts from a bassinette for newborns to a seated stroller for older kids)
- Sling or other baby carrier
- Crib with mattress cover and 2 sheets
- Diapers
- 5–7 diaper covers (see page 108 for a pattern suggestion)
- Cotton wash cloths (See page 124 for a pattern suggestion.)
- Cotton balls (Conventional baby wipes can be too harsh for newborn skin.)
- 4 kimono tops (These are best to use until the umbilical cord falls off.)
- 4 pairs of pants, some of which can be knitted (See page 70 for a pattern suggestion.)
- 3 sleepers (Open dresses make for easier overnight diaper changes. Also try onesies and knitted leg warmers for cool-weather babies; see page 114 for a pattern suggestion.)
- 2–4 blankets
- 2–3 cardigans
- 2–3 hats
- 2–4 pairs of socks
- Personal-care kit that includes scissors, nail clippers, a soft hair brush, and a rectal thermometer (knit the one on page 123.)

    I suggest knitting as many of these items as possible. I found it so fulfilling that the items I used every day were extra special because I had taken time to knit them. Yes, I still go the store to buy baby pajamas. But as a crafter, I think twice before I buy a garment.

BABY SOCKS

Ten toes, ten fingers—the first things we count when we meet our new baby. Relish the simple beauty of a baby's ten little toes, but when it gets cold, warm them up with soft knitted socks. Knit in sportweight yarn and US size 5 needles, this project fits into any purse so you can bring them to the doctor's office and knit as you wait. I did this during my many doctor appointments and learned that I could knit a single sock in about 45 minutes. Challenge yourself, and be ready with socks for baby's first year.

SKILL LEVEL
Intermediate

SIZES
0–6 months (12-18 months, 18-24 months)

FINISHED MEASUREMENTS
Ankle Circumference: 4 (5, 6)" (10 [12.5, 15]cm)

Foot Length: 2¾ (3½, 4¼)" (7 [9, 10.5]cm)

YARN
1 skein of Lorna's Laces Shepherd Sport, 100% superwash wool, 2½ oz (74g), 200 yd (183m) in Happy Valley, (**3**) light

NEEDLES AND NOTIONS
- US size 5 (3.75mm) double-pointed knitting needles.
- Stitch marker
- Yarn needle

GAUGE
24 stitches and 32 rows = 4" (10cm) in stockinette stitch

Adjust needle size as necessary to obtain correct gauge.

NOTES
1. The Baby Socks are is worked in the round on double-pointed knitting needles from the cuff to the toe.
2. Short rows are used to create the heel.
3. The toe stitches are grafted together.

SHORT ROWS
Wrap and turn: Bring yarn to front, slip next stitch, turn, wrap yarn around slip stitch and slip same stitch back onto the right-hand needle. On the next row, work wrapped stitch by picking up wrap and working together with the stitch on the left-hand needle.

CUFF
Cast on 24 (30, 36) stitches and divide evenly among needles. Join to work in the round, being careful not to twist the stitches;

place a marker for the beginning of the round.

Round 1 *K1, p1; repeat from * around.

Repeat round 1 for 4 more rounds.

Work in stockinette stitch until the cuff measures 1½ (2, 2½)" (4 [5, 6.5]cm) from the beginning.

HEEL
Row 1 K12 (15, 18), wrap and turn.
Row 2 P12 (15, 18), wrap and turn.
Row 3 K11 (14, 17), wrap and turn.
Row 4 P10 (13, 16), wrap and turn.
Row 5 K9 (12, 15), wrap and turn.
Row 6 P8 (11, 14), wrap and turn.
Row 7 K7 (10, 13), wrap and turn.
Row 8 P6 (9, 12), wrap and turn.
Row 9 K5 (8, 11), wrap and turn.

For 0–6 Months Size Only
Begin working from row 12, below.

For 12–18 Months and 18–24 Months Sizes Only
Row 10 P -(7, 10), wrap and turn
Row 11 K -(6, 9), wrap and turn.

For All Sizes
Row 12 P5 (5, 8), wrap and turn.
Row 13 K6 (6, 9), wrap and turn.
Row 14 P7, (7, 10), wrap and turn.
Row 15 K8 (8, 11), wrap and turn.
Row 16 P9 (9, 12), wrap and turn.
Row 17 K10 (10, 13), wrap and turn.
Row 18 P11 (11, 14), wrap and turn.
Row 19 K12 (12, 15), wrap and turn.

For 0–6 Months Size Only
Begin working from row 23, below.

For 12–18 Months and 18–24 Months Sizes Only
Row 20 Purl -(13, 16), wrap and turn.
Row 21 Knit -(14, 17), wrap and turn.
Row 22 Purl -(15, 18), wrap and turn.

For All Sizes

Row 23 Place marker for beginning of round, k12 (15, 18), place marker, knit remaining stitches.

Work in stockinette stitch in the round on all the stitches until sock measures 1½ (2, 2½)" (4 [5 6.5]cm) from tip of heel.

TOE

Round 1 *K1, ssk, knit to marker, k2tog, k1; repeat from * around.
Round 2 Knit.
Repeat last 2 rounds 4 (5, 6) more times—4 (6, 8) stitches remain.

Graft Toe Stitches

Divide remaining stitches between 2 needles, and hold the needles parallel to each other.

1. Thread yarn needle with yarn.
2. Set up stitches: Put the yarn needle into the first stitch on the front knitting needle as if to purl, and pull the yarn through. Next, pull the yarn needle through the first stitch on the rear knitting needle as if to knit.
3. Pull the yarn needle through the first stitch on the front knitting needle again as if to knit, and slip the stitch off the knitting needle. Next, pull yarn needle through the second stitch on the front knitting needle as if to purl, but leave this stitch on the knitting needle.
4. Pull the yarn needle through the first stitch on the rear knitting needle as if to purl, and slip the stitch off the knitting needle. Next, pull the yarn needle through the second stitch on the rear knitting needle as if to knit, but leave this stitch on the knitting needle.

Repeat Steps 3 and 4 until all stitches have been worked.

FINISHING

Weave in ends.
Lightly block.

WINTER WONDERLAND HAT

Just like snowflakes, no two babies are alike. This old-fashioned helmet will keep your one-of-a-kind kid warm in any winter wonderland. With this knitted hat, your friends will say that even your baby's accessories are unique.

SKILL LEVEL
Intermediate

SIZES
0–6 months (12 months, 18–24 months)

FINISHED MEASUREMENTS
Head Circumference: 14 (16, 18)" (35.5 [40.5, 45.5]cm)

Snowflake Diameter: 4 (5, 5¾)" (10 [12.5, 14.5]cm)

YARN
1 skein of Karabella Yarns Boise, 50% cashmere, 50% merino wool, 1¾ oz (50g), 163 yd (149m) in #59 Cream, (**2**) fine

NEEDLES AND NOTIONS
- US size 5 (3.75mm) circular knitting needle, long enough to accommodate stitches, or size needed to obtain gauge
- Stitch markers
- Cable needle
- Pom-pom maker
- Yarn needle

GAUGE
26 stitches and 34 rows = 4" (10cm) in stockinette stitch

Adjust needle size as necessary to obtain correct gauge.

NOTES
1. The Hat is knit back and forth in rows on a circular needle to accommodate the large number of stitches.
2. The Hat Band is worked flat. Stitches are then picked up along the long edges and are then incorporated into three of the sides of a Medallion. The Hat is secured with Chin Ties.

ABBREVIATIONS
C2B: Slip next stitch to cable needle and hold in back. Knit the next stitch from the left-hand needle. Return stitch from cable needle to the left-hand needle and purl it.

C2F: Slip next stitch to cable needle and hold in front. Knit the next stitch from the left-hand needle. Return the stitch from the cable needle to the left-hand needle and purl it.

K2tog: (An easy right-slanting decrease.) Knit the next 2 stitches together through the fronts of the loops at the same time.

K2tog tbl: (An easy left-slanting decrease.) Insert the right-hand needle through the backs of the loops of the next 2 stitches at the same time and knit them together.

P3tog: Slip the right-hand needle into the next 3 stitches as if to purl. Purl the stitches together.

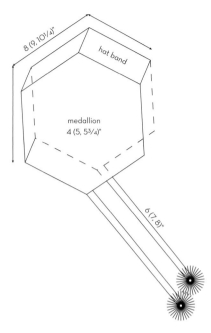

8 (9, 10¼)"

hat band

medallion
4 (5, 5¾)"

6 (7, 8)"

HAT BAND

Cast on 24 stitches. Work in stockinette stitch for 16 rows, ending with a wrong-side row.

Decrease Round (Right Side) K1, k2tog, work to last 3 stitches, k2tog tbl, k1.

Work 7 rows in stockinette stitch.

Repeat the last 8 rows until 18 stitches remain. Continue in stockinette stitch until the piece measures 8 (9, 10¼)" (20.5 [23, 26]cm) from the beginning.

Bind off. Block piece flat.

RIGHT SNOWFLAKE MEDALLION

0–6 Months Size Only

Cast on 27 stitches. Do not turn. With right side facing, starting at the cast-on row and ending at the bind-off row, pick up and knit 61 stitches evenly along the side edge of the Hat Band. Do not turn. Cast on 19 stitches—107 stitches.

Row 1 K2, place a stitch marker on the last stitch worked, knit to last 2 stitches, k1 and place a marker on this stitch, k1. The marked stitches will indicate where to pick up stitches for the Chin Ties.
Row 2 Knit.
Row 3 Knit.
Row 4 K1, *k2tog, p2, k2, p3, k2, p2, k2tog tbl; repeat from * to last stitch, k1—93 stitches.

Row 5 P1, *p1, k2, p2, k3, p2, k2, p1; repeat from * to last stitch, p1.
Row 6 K1, *k2tog, C2B, k1, p3, k1, C2F, k2tog tbl; repeat from * to last stitch, k1—79 stitches.
Row 7 P1, *p2, k1, p1, k3, p1, k1, p2; repeat from * to last stitch, p1.
Row 8 K1, *k2tog, p1, k1, p3, k1, p1, k2tog tbl; repeat from * to last stitch, k1—65 stitches.
Row 9 P1, *p1, k1, p1, k1, p1, k1, p1, k1, p1; repeat from * to last stitch, p1.
Row 10 K1, *k2tog, k1, p1, k1, p1, k1, k2tog tbl; repeat from * to last stitch, k1—51 stitches.
Row 11 P1, *p2, k1, p1, k1, p2; repeat from * to last stitch, p1.
Row 12 K1, *k2tog, p1, k1, p1, k2tog tbl; repeat from * to last stitch, k1—37 stitches.
Row 13 P1, *p1, k1, p1, k1, p1; repeat from * to last stitch, p1.
Row 14 K1, *k2tog, k1, k2tog tbl; repeat from * to last stitch, k1—23 stitches.
Row 15 P1, *p3tog; repeat from * to last stitch, p1—9 stitches.

Cut yarn, leaving a 6" (15cm) tail. Thread the tail through the remaining stitches and pull tight to close. Knot to secure. Use same tail to sew seam closed.

12 Months Size Only

Cast on 32 stitches. Do not turn. With right side facing, starting at the cast-on row and ending at the bind-off row, pick up and knit 68 stitches evenly along the side edge of the Hat Band. Do not turn. Cast on 21 stitches—121 stitches.

Row 1 K2, place a stitch marker on the last stitch worked, knit to last 2 stitches, k1 and place a marker on this stitch, k1. The marked stitches will indicate where to pick up stitches for the Chin Ties.

Row 2 Knit.

Row 3 Knit.

Row 4 K1, *k2tog, p2, k2, p5, k2, p2, k2tog tbl; repeat from * to last stitch, k1—107 stitches.

Row 5 P1, *p1, k2, p2, k5, p2, k2, p1; repeat from * to last stitch, p1.

Row 6 K1, *k2tog, C2B, k1, p5, k1, C2F, k2tog tbl; repeat from * to last stitch, k1—93 stitches.

Row 7 P1, *p2, k1, p1, k5, p1, k1, p2; repeat from * to last stitch, p1.

Row 8 K1, *k2tog, p1, k1, p5, k1, p1, k2tog tbl; repeat from * to last stitch, k1—79 stitches.

Row 9 P1, *p1, k1, p1, k5, p1, k1, p1; repeat from * to last stitch, p1.

Row 10 K1, *k2tog, k1, p1, k1, p1, k1, p1, k1, k2tog tbl; repeat from * to last stitch, k1—65 stitches.

Row 11 P1, *p2, k1, p1, k1, p1, k1, p2; repeat from * to last stitch, p1.

Row 12 K1, *k2tog, p1, k1, p1, k1, p1, k2tog tbl; repeat from * to last stitch, k1—51 stitches.

Row 13 P1, *p1, k1, p1, k1, p1, k1, p1; repeat from * to last stitch, p1.

Row 14 K1, *k2tog, k1, p1, k1, k2tog tbl; repeat from * to last stitch, k1—37 stitches.

Row 15 P1, *p2, k1, p2; repeat from * to last stitch, p1.

Row 16 K1, *k2tog, p1, k2tog tbl; repeat from * to last stitch, k1—23 stitches.

Row 17 P1, *p3tog; repeat from * to last stitch, p1—9 stitches.

Cut yarn, leaving a 6" (15cm) tail. Thread the tail through the remaining stitches and pull tight to close. Knot to secure. Use same tail to sew seam closed.

18–24 Months Size Only
Cast on 47 stitches. Do not turn. With right side facing, starting at the cast-on row and ending at the bind-off row, pick up and knit 79 stitches evenly along the side edge of the Hat Band. Do not turn. Cast on 23 stitches—149 stitches.

Row 1 K2, place a stitch marker on the last stitch worked, knit to last 2 stitches, k1 and place a marker on this stitch, k1. The marked stitches will indicate where to pick up stitches for the Chin Ties.

Row 2 Knit.

Row 3 Knit.

Row 4 K1, * k2tog, p2, k2, p2, k1, p3, k1, p2, k2, p2, k2tog tbl; repeat from * to last stitch, k1—135 stitches.

Row 5 P1, *p1, k2, p2, k2, p1, k3, p1, k2, p2, k2, p1; repeat from * to last stitch, p1.

AS YOU WATCH YOUR BELLY SWELL, take some time to get your hospital bag ready. Here is a short checklist to help you organize your hospital bag.

- Shawl Sweater (page 117)
- Coming-home outfits—for you and for baby
- Comfy undies
- Nursing bras
- At least three newborn diapers
- Makeup
- Knitting
- Book to read
- Journal and pen
- Camera
- Phone list
- Insurance info

Pack the bag and leave it in the hall closet or the nursery—somewhere convenient. While we were waiting for Cole to arrive, I used his nursery as a knitting room and storeroom. I put my hospital bag and a sibling kit (page 92) for Nora inside the doorway so we could grab them both at any time.

Row 6 K1, *k2tog, C2B, k1, p2, k1, p3, k1, p2, k1, C2F, k2tog tbl; repeat from * to last stitch, k1—121 stitches.

Row 7 P1, *p2, k1, p1, k2, p1, k3, p1, k2, p1, k1, p2; repeat from * to last stitch, p1.

Row 8 K1, *k2tog, p1, k1, p2, k1, p3, k1, p2, k1, p1, k2tog tbl; repeat from * to last stitch, k1—107 stitches.

Row 9 P1, *p1, k1, p1, k2, p1, k3, p1, k2, p1, k1, p1; repeat from * to last stitch, p1.

Row 10 K1, *k2tog, k1, p1, C2B, p3, C2F, p1, k1, k2tog tbl; repeat from * to last stitch, k1—93 stitches.

Row 11 P1, *p2, k1, p1, k5, p1, k1, p2; repeat from * to last stitch, p1.

Row 12 K1, *k2tog, p1, k1, p2, k1, p2, k1, p1, k2tog tbl; repeat from * to last stitch, k1—79 stitches.

Row 13 P1, *p1, k1, p1, k2, p1, k2, p1, k1, p1; repeat from * to last stitch, p1.

Row 14 K1, *k2tog, k1, p2, k1, p2, k, k2tog tbl; repeat from * to last stitch, k1—65 stitches.

Row 15 P1, *p2, k2, p1, k2, p2; repeat from * to last stitch, p1.

Row 16 K1, *k2tog, p2, k1, p2, k2tog tbl; repeat from * to last stitch, k1—51 stitches.

Row 17 P1, *p1, k2, p1, k2, p1; repeat from * to last stitch, p1.

Row 18 K1, *k2tog, p1, k1, p1, k2togtbl; repeat from * to last stitch, k1—37 stitches.

Row 19 P1, *p1, k1, p1, k1, p1; repeat from * to last stitch, p1.

Row 20 K1, *k2tog, k1, k2togtbl; repeat from * to last stitch, k1—23 stitches.

Row 21 P1, *p3tog; repeat from * to last stitch, p1—9 stitches.

Cut yarn, leaving a 6" (15cm) tail. Thread the tail through the remaining stitches and pull tight to close. Knot to secure. Use same tail and sew seam closed.

LEFT SNOWFLAKE MEDALLION

0–6 Months Size Only

Cast on 19 stitches. Do not turn. With right side facing, starting at the bind-off row and ending at the cast-on row, pick up and knit 61 stitches evenly along the side edge of the Hat Band. Do not turn. Cast on 27 stitches—107 stitches.

Row 1 K2, place a stitch marker on the last stitch worked, knit to last 2 stitches, k1 and place a marker on this stitch, k1. The marked stitches will indicate where to pick up stitches for the Chin Ties.

Row 2 Knit.

Row 3 Knit.

Row 4 K1, *k2tog, p2, k2, p3, k2, p2, k2tog tbl; repeat from * to last stitch, k1—93 stitches.

Row 5 P1, *p1, k2, p2, k3, p2, k2, p1; repeat from * to last stitch, p1.

Row 6 K1, *k2tog, C2B, k1, p3, k1, C2F, k2tog tbl; repeat from * to last stitch, k1—79 stitches.

Row 7 P1, *p2, k1, p1, k3, p1, k1, p2; repeat from * to last stitch, p1.

Row 8 K1, *k2tog, p1, k1, p3, k1, p1, k2tog tbl; repeat from * to last stitch, k1—65 stitches.

Row 9 P1, *p1, k1, p1, k1, p1, k1, p1, k1, p1; repeat from * to last stitch, p1.

Row 10 K1, *k2tog, k1, p1, k1, p1, k1, k2tog tbl; repeat from * to last stitch, k1—51 stitches.

Row 11 P1, *p2, k1, p1, k1, p2; repeat from * to last stitch, p1.

Row 12 K1, *k2tog, p1, k1, p1, k2tog tbl; repeat from * to last stitch, k1—37 stitches.

Row 13 P1, *p1, k1, p1, k1, p1; repeat from * to last stitch, p1.

Row 14 K1, *k2tog, k1, k2tog tbl; repeat from * to last stitch, k1—23 stitches.

Row 15 P1, *p3tog; repeat from * to last stitch, p1—9 stitches.

Cut yarn, leaving a 6" (15cm) tail. Thread the tail through the remaining stitches and pull tight to close. Knot to secure. Use same tail to sew seam closed.

Cast on 21 stitches. Do not turn. With right side facing, starting at the bind-off row and ending at the cast-on row, pick up and knit 68 stitches evenly along the side edge of the Hat Band. Do not turn. Cast on 32 stitches—121 stitches.

Row 1 K2, place a stitch marker on the last stitch worked, knit to last 2 stitches, k1 and place a marker on this stitch, k1. The marked stitches will indicate where to pick up stitches for the Chin Ties.

Row 2 Knit.

Row 3 Knit.

Row 4 K1, *k2tog, p2, k2, p5, k2, p2, k2tog tbl; repeat from * to last stitch, k1—107 stitches.

Row 5 P1, *p1, k2, p2, k5, p2, k2, p1; repeat from * to last stitch, p1.

Row 6 K1, *k2tog, C2B, k1, p5, k1, C2F, k2tog tbl; repeat from * to last stitch, k1—93 stitches.

Row 7 P1, *p2, k1, p1, k5, p1, k1, p2; repeat from * to last stitch, p1.

Row 8 K1, *k2tog, p1, k1, p5, k1, p1, k2tog tbl; repeat from * to last stitch, k1—79 stitches.

Row 9 P1, *p1, k1, p1, k5, p1, k1, p1; repeat from * to last stitch, p1.

Row 10 K1, *k2tog, k1, p1, k1, p1, k1, p1, k1, k2tog tbl; repeat from * to last stitch, k1—65 stitches.

Row 11 P1, *p2, k1, p1, k1, p1, k1, p2; repeat from * to last stitch, p1.

Row 12 K1, *k2tog, p1, k1, p1, k1, p1, k2tog tbl; repeat from * to last stitch, k1—51 stitches.

Row 13 P1, *p1, k1, p1, k1, p1, k1, p1; repeat from * to last stitch, p1.

Row 14 K1, *k2tog, k1, p1, k1, k2tog tbl; repeat from * to last stitch, k1—37 stitches.

Row 15 P1, *p2, k1, p2; repeat from * to last stitch, p1.

Row 16 K1, *k2tog, p1, k2tog tbl; repeat from * to last stitch, k1—23 stitches.

Row 17 P1, *p3tog; repeat from * to last stitch, p1—9 stitches.

Cut yarn, leaving a 6" (15cm) tail. Thread the tail through the remaining stitches and pull tight to close. Knot to secure. Use same tail to sew seam closed.

Cast on 23 stitches. Do not turn. With right side facing, starting at the cast-on row and ending at the bind-off row, pick up and knit 79 stitches evenly along the side edge of the Hat Band. Do not turn. Cast on 47 stitches—149 stitches.

Row 1 K2, place a stitch marker on the last stitch worked, knit to last 2 stitches, k1 and place a marker on this stitch, k1. Marked stitches will indicate where to pick up stitches for Chin Ties.

Row 2 Knit.

Row 3 Knit.

Row 4 K1, * k2tog, p2, k2, p2, k1, p3, k1, p2, k2, p2, k2tog tbl; repeat from * to last stitch, k1—135 stitches.

Row 5 P1, *p1, k2, p2, k2, p1, k3, p1, k2, p2, k2, p1; repeat from * to last stitch, p1.

Row 6 K1, *k2tog, C2B, k1, p2, k1, p3, k1, p2, k1, C2F, k2tog tbl; repeat from * to last stitch, k1—121 stitches.

Row 7 P1, *p2, k1, p1, k2, p1, k3, p1, k2, p1, k1, p2; repeat from * to last stitch, p1.

Row 8 K1, *k2tog, p1, k1, p2, k1, p3, k1, p2, k1, p1, k2tog tbl; repeat from * to last stitch, k1—107 stitches.

Row 9 P1, *p1, k1, p1, k2, p1, k3, p1, k2, p1, k1, p1; repeat from * to last stitch, p1.

Row 10 K1, *k2tog, k1, p1, C2B, p3, C2F, p1, k1, k2tog tbl; repeat from * to last stitch, k1—93 stitches.

Row 11 P1, *p2, k1, p1, k5, p1, k1, p2; repeat from * to last stitch, p1.

Row 12 K1, *k2tog, p1, k1, p2, k1, p2, k1, p1, k2tog tbl; repeat from * to last stitch, k1—79 stitches.

Row 13 P1, *p1, k1, p1, k2, p1, k2, p1, k1, p1; repeat from * to last stitch, p1.

Row 14 K1, *k2tog, k1, p2, k1, p2, k, k2tog tbl; repeat from * to last stitch, k1—65 stitches.

Row 15 P1, *p2, k2, p1, k2, p2; repeat from * to last stitch, p1.

Row 16 K1, *k2tog, p2, k1, p2, k2tog tbl; repeat from * to last stitch, k1—51 stitches.

Row 17 P1, *p1, k2, p1, k2, p1; repeat from * to last stitch, p1.

Row 18 K1, *k2tog, p1, k1, p1, k2togtbl; repeat from * to last stitch, k1—37 stitches.

Row 19 P1, *p1, k1, p1, k1, p1; repeat from * to last stitch, p1.

Row 20 K1, *k2tog, k1, k2togtbl; repeat from * to last stitch, k1—23 stitches.

Row 21 P1, *p3tog; repeat from * to last stitch, p1—9 stitches.

Cut yarn, leaving a 6" (15cm) tail. Thread the tail through the remaining stitches and pull tight to close. Knot to secure. Use same tail to sew seam closed.

CHIN TIES

With right side facing, pick up and knit 4 stitches between the markers on one Snowflake Medallion. Work in stockinette stitch for 6 (7, 8)" (15 [18, 20.5]cm). Bind off. Repeat on opposite Snowflake Medallion.

FINISHING

Weave in ends.

Make 2 pom-poms 3" (7.5cm) in diameter accrording to the manufacturer's insructions for the pom-pom maker. Attach a pom-pom to the end of each Chin Tie.

THINK SPRING HAT

This soft pink hat with embroidered flowers celebrates the joys of spring but still keeps your baby's head warm on those chilly early spring days. It is knit in the softest alpaca—you may even want to make one for yourself.

SKILL LEVEL
Easy

SIZES
0-6 months (12 months, 18 months, 24 months)

FINISHED MEASUREMENTS
Head Circumference: 13½ (15½, 18½, 20)" (34.5 [39.5, 47, 51]cm)

YARN
1 skein of Blue Sky Alpacas Melange, 100% baby alpaca, 1¾ oz (50g), 110 yd (100m) in #810 Cotton Candy (A), **2** fine

1 ball each of Madil Kid Seta, 70% kid mohair, 30% silk, ¾ oz (25g), 230 yd (210m) in #403 Aqua (B) and #460 Salmon (C), **5** bulky

1 ball of Rowan KidSilk Night, 67% super kid mohair, 18% silk, 10% polyester, 5% nylon, ¾ oz (25g), 227 yd (208m) in #607 Starlight (D), **4** medium

NEEDLES AND NOTIONS
- US size 3 (3.25mm) set of double-pointed knitting needles, or size needed to obtain gauge
- Stitch markers
- Yarn needle

GAUGE
26 stitches and 32 rows = 4" (10cm) in stockinette stitch

Adjust needle size as necessary to obtain correct gauge.

NOTE
The Hat is worked in rounds on double-pointed knitting needles.

HAT
With A, cast on 88 (100, 120, 130) stitches and divide evenly among needles. Place marker and join, taking care not to twist stitches.

Round 1 (K1, p1) around for ribbing.

Work in ribbing for 1 (1, 1¼, 1½)" (2.5[2.5, 3, 4]cm) from beginning.

Change to stockinette stitch and work until the piece measures 3½ (4, 4¾, 5½)" (9 [10, 12, 14]cm) from the beginning.

SHAPE CROWN
Round 1 *K6 (8, 10, 11), k2tog tbl; repeat from * around—77 (90, 110, 120) stitches.
Round 2 Knit.
Round 3 *K5 (7, 9, 10), k2tog tbl; repeat from * around—66 (80, 100, 110) stitches.
Round 4 Knit.
Round 5 *K4 (6, 8, 9), k2tog tbl; repeat from * around—55 (70, 90, 100) stitches.
Round 6 Knit.

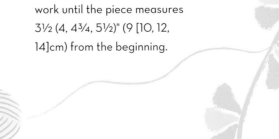

Round 7 *K3, (5, 7, 8), k2tog tbl; repeat from * around—44 (60, 80, 90) stitches.

Round 8
For 0–6 months size only *K2, k2tog tbl; repeat from * around—33 stitches.
For all other sizes Knit.

Round 9
*K1 (4, 6, 7), k2tog tbl; repeat from * around—22 (50, 70, 80) stitches.

Round 10
For 0–6 months size only (K2tog tbl) around—11 stitches. Cut yarn, leaving a long end. Pull end through stitches and pull tightly to close. Knot to secure.
For all other sizes *K- (3, 5, 6), k2tog tbl; repeat from * around— - (40, 60, 70) stitches.

Round 11 *K- (2, 4, 5), k2tog tbl; repeat from * around— - (30, 50, 60) stitches.
Round 12 *K- (1, 3, 4), k2tog tbl; repeat from * around— - (20, 40, 50) stitches.

Round 13
For 12 months size only (K2tog tbl) around—10 stitches. Cut yarn, leaving a long end. Pull end through stitches and pull tightly to close. Knot to secure.
For all other sizes *K- (-, 2, 3), k2tog tbl; repeat from * around— (-, 30, 40) stitches.

Round 14 *K- (-, 1, 2), k2tog tbl; repeat from * around— - (-, 20, 30) stitches.

Round 15
For 18 months size only (K2tog tbl) around—10 stitches. Cut yarn, leaving a long end. Pull end through stitches and pull tightly to close. Knot to secure.
For 24 months size only *K1, k2tog tbl; repeat from * around—20 stitches.

Round 16 (K2tog tbl) around—10 stitches. Cut yarn, leaving a long end. Pull end through stitches and pull tightly to close. Knot to secure.

FINISHING

Using B, C, and D, embroider flowers in varying sizes in lazy daisy stitch as in the photograph.

Weave in ends. Lightly block.

SUMMER LOVING HAT

Grab the sunblock! This fun summer hat, a quick knit in one of my favorite cottons, protects your baby's eyes and sensitive skin. Make a couple to have a full set of accessories in your summer baby's wardrobe.

SKILL LEVEL Easy

SIZES
0–6 months (12 months, 18 months, 24 months)

FINISHED MEASUREMENTS
Head Circumference: 13½ (15½, 18½, 20)" (34.5 [39.5, 47, 51]cm)

YARN
1 skein of Blue Sky Alpacas Dyed Cotton, 100% organically grown cotton, 3½ oz (100g), 150 yd (137m) in #616 Sky, (4) medium

NEEDLES AND NOTIONS
- US size 8 (5mm) knitting needles, or size needed to obtain gauge
- US size 8 (5mm) double-pointed knitting needles
- Stitch markers
- Yarn needle

GAUGE
16 stitches and 24 rows = 4" (10cm) in stockinette stitch.

Adjust needle size as necessary to obtain correct gauge.

NOTE
The Hat is worked back and forth in rows and sewn together along a back seam.

HAT

Cast on 52 (62, 72, 82) stitches. Work in stockinette stitch for 2¾ (3, 3¾, 4)" (7 [7.5, 9.5, 10]cm), ending with a right-side row.

SHAPE CROWN

Next Row (Wrong Side) Knit.
Decrease Row K1 *k3, k2tog; repeat from * to last stitch, k1—42 (50, 58, 66) stitches.
Knit 3 rows.

Decrease Row K1, *k2, k2tog; repeat from * to last stitch, k1—32 (38, 44, 50) stitches.
Knit 3 rows.

Decrease Row K1, *k1, k2tog; repeat from * to last stitch, k1—22 (26, 30, 34) stitches.
Knit 3 rows.

Decrease Row K1, *k2tog; repeat from * to last stitch, k1—12 (14, 16, 18) stitches.
Knit 1 row.

Decrease Row K1, k2tog; repeat from * to last stitch, k1—7 (8, 9, 10) stitches.

Cut yarn, leaving a long tail. Pull end through stitches tightly to close. Knot to secure.

FINISHING

Sew back seam.

BRIM

Cast on 20 (20, 22, 22) stitches. Knit 2 rows.

Next Row (Right Side) K2, M1, knit to last 2 stitches, M1, k2.
Next Row K2, purl to last 2 stitches, k2.

Repeat last 2 rows 3 (3, 3, 4) times—26 (26, 28, 30) stitches.

Next Row Knit.
Next Row K2, purl to last 2 stitches, k2.

Repeat the last 2 rows once more.

With the right side facing, cast on 3 stitches at the beginning of the row.
1. Knit these 3 stitches plus 1 (4 stitches worked).
2. Pass the second-to-last stitch over the last knitted stitch on the right-hand needle (1 stitch bound off).
3. Slip the 3 stitches from the right-hand needle back to the left-hand needle.

Repeat steps 1–3 until all Brim stitches are bound off.

Sew Brim, centered, on the front of the Hat.

Weave in ends. Lightly block.

AUTUMN HOMECOMING HAT

This alpaca striped hat reminds me of homecoming football games, falling leaves, and cool breezes. When I had Nora and Cole, the term "homecoming" gained a whole new meaning. This hat is sure to warm up any baby and make homecoming so much more special.

SKILL LEVEL
Easy

SIZES
0–6 months (12 months, 18 months, 24 months)

FINISHED MEASUREMENTS
Head Circumference: 13½ (15½, 18½, 20)" (34.5 [39.5, 47, 51]cm)

YARN
- 1 skein each of Blue Sky Alpacas Sport Weight, 100% baby alpaca, 1¾ oz (50g), 110 yd (100m) in #522 Denim (A) and #504 Natural Light Tan (C), **2** fine
- 1 skein of Blue Sky Alpacas Melange, 100% baby alpaca, 1¾ oz (50g), 110 yd (100m) in #802 Pesto (B), **2** fine

NEEDLES AND NOTIONS
- US size 3 (3.25mm) set of double-pointed knitting needles, or size needed to obtain gauge
- Stitch markers
- Yarn needle

GAUGE
26 stitches and 32 rows = 4" (10cm) in stockinette stitch

Adjust needle size as necessary to obtain correct gauge.

NOTE

The Hat is worked in rounds on double-pointed knitting needles.

HAT

With A, cast on 88 (100, 120, 130) stitches and divide evenly among needles. Place marker and join, taking care not to twist the stitches.

Round 1 (K1, p1) around for ribbing.

Work in ribbing for 1 (1, 1¼, 1½)" (2.5 [2.5, 3, 4]cm) from the beginning.

Work in stockinette stitch for 1 (1½, 1¾, 2)" (2.5 [4, 4.5, 5]cm).

Change to C and purl 1 round.

Change to B and knit 9 rounds. Cut B.

Change to C and purl 1 round. Cut C.

Change to A and knit until the piece measures 3½ (4, 4¾, 5½)" (9 [10, 12, 14]cm) from the beginning.

Shape Crown

Round 1 *K6 (8, 10, 11), k2tog; repeat from * around—77 (90, 110, 120) stitches.

Round 2 Knit.
Round 3 *K5 (7, 9, 10), k2tog; repeat from * around—66 (80, 100, 110) stitches.
Round 4 Knit.
Round 5 *K4 (6, 8, 9), k2tog; repeat from * around—55 (70, 90, 100) stitches.
Round 6 Knit.
Round 7 *K3, (5, 7, 8), k2tog; repeat from * around—44 (60, 80, 90) stitches.

Round 8
For 0-6 months size only *K2, k2tog; repeat from * around—33 stitches.
For all other sizes Knit.

Round 9 *K1 (4, 6, 7), k2tog; repeat from * around—22 (50, 70, 80) stitches.

Round 10
For 0-6 months size only (K2tog) around—11 stitches. Cut yarn, leaving a long tail. Pull end through stitches and pull tightly to close. Knot to secure.
For all other sizes *K- (3, 5, 6), k2tog; repeat from * around— - (40, 60, 70) stitches.

Round 11 *K- (2, 4, 5), k2tog; repeat from * around— - (30, 50, 60) stitches.

Round 12 *K- (1, 3, 4), k2tog; repeat from * around— - (20, 40, 50) stitches.

Round 13
For 12 months size only (K2tog) around—10 stitches. Cut yarn, leaving a long tail. Pull end through stitches and pull tightly to close. Knot to secure.
For all other sizes *K- (-, 2, 3); k2tog; repeat from * around— - (-, 30, 40) stitches.

Round 14 *K- (-, 1, 2), k2tog; repeat from * around— - (-, 20, 30) stitches.

Round 15
For 18 months size only (K2tog) around—10 stitches. Cut yarn, leaving a long tail. Pull end through stitches and pull tightly to close. Knot to secure.
For 24 months size only *K1, k2tog; repeat from * around—20 stitches.

Round 16 (K2tog) around—10 stitches. Cut yarn, leaving a long tail. Pull end through stitches and pull tightly to close. Knot to secure.

FINISHING

Weave in ends. Lightly block.

The Big Event

AS YOU PACK YOUR BAGS, develop your birth plan. It is a list of your priorities for the birth experience. But remember, as with many parts of pregnancy, this plan is only a guide to the day. Be flexible. You can't control the birth completely. The best part of preparing a birth plan is the forethought you put into one of life's most important experiences. Truthfully, I did not have a thorough birth plan for Nora or Cole. I had only two requests: I wanted an epidural to help manage the pain, and only Alan could be in the room during the actual birth.

Here are some basic questions that you should consider as you develop your birth plan.

1. Birth partners: Who do you want to participate in the experience?

2. Environment: Where do you want to give birth?

3. Pain relief: How do you want to manage the pain?

4. Interventions: How do you want to cope with birth issues such as breaking water, forceps, and episiotomies?

5. Birthing: What positions do you want to use while giving birth?

6. Postdelivery: What should happen once the baby has arrived?

Discuss your feelings and choices with your partner, family members, and health-care provider. I wish you all the best for your birth experience. Good luck!

BABY SHOWER
EASY SWATCH BL...

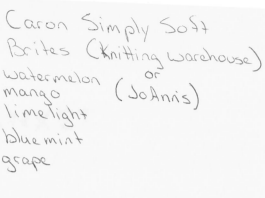

*Caron Simply Soft
Brites (Knitting warehouse)
or (JoAnns)
watermelon
mango
limelight
blue mint
grape*

There is no need for silly games like Guess...
shower. Instead, throw a knitted baby show...
cotton square. Garter stitch squares are s...
do it. The more accomplished knitter can ...
intricate stitch patterns. As long as they a... ... ...
end, the sky is the limit.

SKILL LEVEL
All levels

FINISHED MEASUREMENTS
22½" (57cm) wide by 22½" (57cm)

YARN
1 skein of Blue Sky Alpacas Dyed
Cotton, 100% organically grown
cotton, 3½ oz (100g), 150 yd
(137m) in #601 Poppy, #633 Pickle,
#632 Mediterranean, #619 Tomato,
and #618 Orchid (D), (**4**) medium

NEEDLES AND NOTIONS
- US size 8 (5mm) knitting
  needles, or size needed to
  obtain gauge
- Yarn needle

GAUGE
16 stitches and 20 rows = 4"
(10cm) in stockinette stitch

Adjust needle size as necessary
to obtain correct gauge.

NOTES
1. The Blanket consists of
   25 squares, each 4½"
   (11.5cm).
2. Make 5 squares in each color
   in a variety of stitches.
3. Use the stitch patterns given
   here, or try some of your
   favorites.
4. The stitch patterns for each of
   the squares are on page 152.
   Feel free to follow the text or
   the charts.

GARTER STITCH SQUARE
Cast on 20 stitches. Knit every
row until the piece measures
4½" (11.5cm) from the beginning.

Bind off.

**STOCKINETTE STITCH
SQUARE**
Cast on 20 stitches.

Row 1 Knit.

Row 2 Purl.

Repeat rows 1 and 2 until the
piece measures 4½" (11.5cm)
from the beginning.

Bind off in pattern.

STITCH KEY

☐ = K on right side, p on wrong side

⊡ = P on right side, k on wrong side

BASKETWEAVE STITCH SQUARE

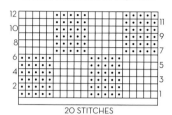

20 STITCHES

MOCK CABLE SQUARE

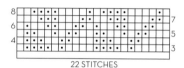

22 STITCHES

DIAGONAL RIB

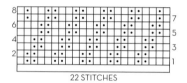

22 STITCHES

TRIANGLE RIB

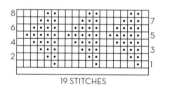

19 STITCHES

GATEPOSTS

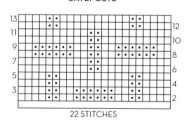

22 STITCHES

BASKETWEAVE STITCH SQUARE

Cast on 20 stitches.

Row 1 *K5, p5; repeat from * across.

Rows 2–6 Repeat row 1.

Row 7 *P5, k5; repeat from * across.

Rows 8–12 Repeat row 7.

Bind off in pattern.

MOCK CABLE SQUARE

Cast on 22 stitches.

Row 1 Knit.

Row 2 Purl.

Row 3 K1, *k4, p1, k1, p4; repeat from * once more, k1.

Row 4 P1, *k3, p2, k2, p3; repeat from * once more, p1.

Row 5 K1, *k2, p2, k1, p1, k2, p2; repeat from * once more, k1.

Row 6 P1, *k1, p2, k2, p2, k2, p1; repeat from * once more, p1.

Row 7 K1, *p2, k3, p3, k2; repeat from * once more, k1.

Row 8 P1, *p1, k4, p4, k1; repeat from * once more, p1.

Repeat rows 3–8 four more times.

Bind off knitwise.

DIAGONAL RIB SQUARE

Cast on 22 stitches.

Row 1 K1, *k2, p2; repeat from *, k1.

Row 2 P1, *k2, p2; repeat from *, p1.

Row 3 K2, *p2, k2; repeat from *.

Row 4 P2, *k2, p2; repeat from *.

Row 5 K1, *p2, k2; repeat from *, k1.

Row 6 P1, *p2, k2; repeat from *, p1.

Row 7 K1, p1, *k2, p2; repeat from *, end k2, p1, k1.

Row 8 P1, k1, *p2, k2; rep from *, end p2, k1, p1.

Repeat rows 1–8 two more times, then rows 1–6.

Bind off knitwise.

TRIANGLE RIB SQUARE

Cast on 19 stitches.

Row 1 Knit.

Row 2 Purl.

Row 3 K1, *p1, k5; repeat from *.

Row 4 *P4, k2; repeat from *, p1.

Row 5 K1, *p3, k3; repeat from *.

Row 6 *P2, k4; repeat from *, p1.

Row 7 K1, *p5, k1; repeat from *.

Row 8 *P2, k4; repeat from *, p1.

Row 9 K1, *p3, k3; repeat from *.

Row 10 *P4, k2; repeat from *, p1.

Repeat rows 3–10 twice more.

Row 27 Knit.

Row 28 Purl.

Bind off knitwise.

GATEPOSTS SQUARE

Cast on 22 stitches.

Row 1 (Wrong Side) Purl.

Row 2 K4, p2, k2, p6, k2, p2, k4.

Row 3 P4, k2, p2, k6, p2, k2, p4.

Row 4 K4, p2, k10, p2, k4.

Row 5 P4, k2, p10, k2, p4.

Row 6 K10, p2, k10.

Row 7 P10, k2, p10.

Row 8 K2, p6, k2, p2, k2, p6, k2.

Row 9 P2, k6, p2, k2, p2, k6, p2.

Row 10 Repeat row 6.

Row 11 Repeat row 7.

Row 12 Repeat row 4.

Row 13 Repeat row 5.

Rows 14–25 Repeat rows 2–13.

Row 26 Repeat row 2.

Row 27 Repeat row 3.

Row 28 Repeat row 4.

Row 29 Repeat row 5.

Knit 1 row.

Bind off purlwise.

BLANKET

Make 25 squares total, each 4½" (11.5cm). Make 5 squares of each color, using a variety of stitches.

FINISHING

Block squares to 4½" (11.5cm) square. Arrange the squares into the blanket, 5 squares wide by 5 squares long, mixing and matching colors and patterns. Sew together. Weave in ends.

A Knitting Primer

MY MOM TAUGHT ME TO KNIT when I was about nine years old. Girl Scouts and a family friend, Mrs. Hunter, reinforced Mom's lessons. Having grown up in Ireland, my mom knitted English, or Irish, style, also known as "throwing" the yarn. Since she taught me, this is the way I knit, too. Many people ask me to teach them the more efficient way of knitting, Continental knitting. Instead, I tell people just to learn how to knit more relaxed. It's not a competition. Knitting should be calming and pleasing. Knit however you want—just knit.

THE BASICS

Cast On

For most projects in this book, I suggest the long-tail cast-on method. It provides a flexible knitted edge. The only downfall of this method is estimating how long the tail should be. I recommend leaving ½" to 1" (1.3–2.5cm) of yarn for every stitch, less for fine yarns and more for thick yarns.

1. Leave a sufficient amount of yarn to cast on the necessary stitches, and create a slip knot.
2. Place the slip knot on the needle, and place the needle in your right hand.
3. Let the yarn tail and yarn from the ball fall from the slip knot. With your left hand, grab the yarn with three fingers. Place your thumb and index finger between the two strands.
4. Spread your thumb and index finger.
5. Turn your left hand up to show your palm. The yarn should now form a sling shot.
6. Place the needle (in your right hand) through the lower part of the loop formed on your left thumb.
7. Point the needle over the yarn held by your index finger and grab it by pulling the needle down.
8. Pull your thumb over the needle and release the yarn from your thumb (1 stitch cast on).

Repeat steps 3–8 until you have cast on all the stitches for your project. Remember, the slip knot counts as the first stitch.

The Knit Stitch

There is an old knitting rhyme that goes like this: "In through the front door, once around the back, peek through the window, and off jumps Jack." Try out this version of the rhyme as you knit your baby's sweaters, blankets, and socks: "In the front door, grab a blanket, wrap the baby warm and snug, just a nose peeking out, off for a stroll we go!" Either way, here are the basic steps you need to knit.

1. Place the needle with stitches in your left hand, and pick up the empty needle with your right hand. The working yarn should be behind the needles.
2. Put the right-hand needle into the front of the loop of the first stitch from left to right.

3. Wrap the yarn counter-clockwise around the right-hand needle.
4. With the yarn wrapped around your right-hand needle, gently pull the right-hand needle back through the same stitch to create a new stitch.
5. Pull the worked stitch off the left-hand needle.

Repeat steps 2–5 to the end.

The Purl Stitch

The purl stitch complements the knit stitch. The most important thing to remember is that the yarn should be in front of the work as you purl the stitches.

1. Place the needle with stitches in your left hand, and pick up the empty needle with your right hand. The working yarn should be in front of the needles.
2. Put the right-hand needle into the front of the loop of the first stitch, from right to left. The right-hand needle should point to the left.
3. Wrap the yarn counter-clockwise around the right-hand needle.
4. With the yarn wrapped around your right-hand needle, gently pull the right-hand needle back through the same stitch to create a new stitch. The needle will be pulled out to the back of the work.
5. Pull the worked stitch off the left-hand needle. Repeat steps 2–5 to the end.

Binding Off

1. Work the first 2 stitches of the row.
2. Take the left-hand needle and place it into the front of the first worked stitch on the right-hand needle.
3. Gently pull the first worked stitch over the second stitch on the right-hand needle and drop it off the needle. 1 stitch bound off.
4. Work 1 more stitch from the left-hand needle.
5. Repeat steps 2–4 until all the stitches are bound off.

BEYOND THE BASICS

Reading Charts

Some of the advanced projects in this book use charts to demonstrate lace, cable, or intarsia patterns. When you are knitting, charts are like road maps. Maps have legends, keys, and landmarks to help you navigate your way. Knitting charts have similar elements. There is a legend and key to the chart's abbreviations (symbols). There are landmarks such as right-side rows and wrong-side rows. One general rule of thumb is that right-side rows are read from right to left, and wrong-side rows are read from left to right. But before starting a pattern, take a moment get familiar with your chart. Then use that road map to arrive at a beautiful knitted piece.

Yarn Over

When working in the knit stitch: Bring the yarn to the front of your work. Start the next knit stitch and bring the yarn over the right-hand needle to complete the stitch.

When working in the purl stitch: Bring the yarn to the back of the work, start the next purl stitch, bringing the yarn over the right-hand needle to complete the stitch.

Short Row Shaping

The wrap-and-turn technique is used to create short row shaping in many projects, including socks (pages 87 and 130), diaper covers (page 108), and leggings (page 70). Short rows give a little more room without adding length, for example, to add a little extra room in the rear for a full diaper.

Wrap and turn: Bring yarn to front, slip next stitch, turn work, wrap yarn around slipped stitch, and slip same stitch back onto the right-hand needle. On the next row, work wrapped stitch by picking up wrap and working it together with the stitch on the left-hand needle.

Grafting

Divide remaining stitches between 2 needles, and hold the needles parallel to each other.

1. Thread yarn needle with yarn.
2. **Set up stitches:** Put the yarn needle into the first stitch on the front knitting needle as if to purl, and pull the yarn through. Next, pull the yarn needle through the first stitch on the rear knitting needle as if to knit.
3. Pull the yarn needle through the first stitch on the front knitting needle as if to knit, and slip the stitch off the knitting needle. Next, pull yarn needle through the second stitch on the front knitting needle as if to purl, but leave this stitch on the knitting needle.
4. Pull the yarn needle through the first stitch on the rear knitting needle as if to purl, and slip the stitch off the knitting needle. Next, pull the yarn needle through the second stitch on the rear knitting needle as if to knit, but leave this stitch on the knitting needle.

Repeat Steps 3 and 4 until all stitches have been worked.

Intarsia

Intarsia is a method of working different colors in a single row. The key to this method is that you use a different ball of yarn for each color. I suggest using bobbins for each color. To change color, pick up the new color from under the old color to twist the yarns to prevent holes.

Blocking

What is blocking? This is a question I hear every day.

I was taught to steam-block most items. Invest in a good steam iron. But there are other ways to block. It depends on the knitted piece and the desired effect. Here are some basic rules that I follow as I knit. Just remember, if in doubt, try the steam iron first. Then if you need a little more or desire a slightly different effect, try spritzing or soaking the piece.

1. **Lace patterns:** Spritz the knitted piece with water and then pin to desired measurements. Let dry flat.
2. **Cables, ribbing, and other raised stitch patterns:** This is a personal choice. For Her First Party Dress (page 36), I chose to soak the dress and let it dry flat. This softened the cable along the yoke. On the other hand, for the Shawl Collar Sweater (page 82), I

steamed the sweater pieces but did not steam the collar, as I wanted the ribbing to stand firmer. Steam-block first, and if you don't get the desired effect, soak the piece.
3. **Stockinette stitch:** Lay the knitted piece flat between two damp cloths. Lightly run the steam iron over the knitted piece.

Seaming

The most versatile seaming method is mattress stitch. It makes an invisible seam that runs along the selvedge stitches. Simply lay the two pieces flat with right sides facing. Thread a yarn needle. Pull the yarn between the first two stitches on the right piece. Pull the thread over to the left piece and pull the needle through the first two stitches. Continue working the piece, grabbing the ladders between the first and second stitches on each side. Pull tightly to close the seam.

ABBREVIATIONS

C2B: Slip next stitch to cable needle and hold in back. Knit the next stitch from the left-hand needle. Return stitch from cable needle to the left-hand needle and purl it.

C2F: Slip next stitch to cable needle and hold in front. Knit the next stitch from the left-hand needle. Return the stitch from the cable needle to the left-hand needle and purl it.

C4F: Slip next 2 stitches to a cable needle and hold in front. Knit the next 2 stitches from the left-hand needle. Knit the stitches from the cable needle.

C6B: Slip next 3 stitches to cable needle and hold in back. Knit the next 3 stitches from the left-hand needle. Knit the stitches from the cable needle.

C6F: Slip next 3 stitches to cable needle and hold in front. Knit the next 3 stitches from the left-hand needle. Knit the stitches from the cable needle.

K: Knit.

K2tog: This is a right slanting decrease. Knit the next 2 stitches on the left-hand needle together—1 stitch decreased.

K2togtbl: This is a left-slanting decrease. Knit the next 2 stitches on the left-hand needle together through the back loops—1 stitch decreased.

K(nit) 1 f(ront) &b(ack): This is an easy increase stitch. Knit into the next stitch, but before removing it from the left-hand needle, knit again into the back loop of the same stitch. Remove the stitch from the left-hand needle—1 stitch increased.

M(ake) 1 L(eft) (left-leaning increase): Find the horizontal bar between the last completed stitch on the right-hand needle and the next stitch on the left-hand needle. Using the left-hand needle, pick up the horizontal bar by inserting the left-hand needle from back to front. Knit the raised bar through the front loop. (**Hint:** If you have a hole, you may have knit the raised bar through the back loop.)

M(ake) 1 R(ight) (right-leaning increase): Find the horizontal bar between the last completed stitch on the right-hand needle and the next stitch on the left-hand needle. Using the left-hand needle, pick up the horizontal bar by inserting the left-hand needle from front to back. Knit the raised bar through the back loop. (**Hint:** If you have a hole, you may have knit the raised bar through the front loop.)

P: Purl.

P3tog: Purl the next 3 stitches on the left-hand needle together—2 stitches decreased.

P(url) 1f(ront) &b(ack): This is an easy increase stitch. Purl into the next stitch, but before removing it from the left-hand needle, purl again into the back loop of the same stitch. Remove the stitch from the left-hand needle—1 stitch increased.

P(ass) S(lipped) S(titch) O(ver): This is a left-slanting decrease. Slip the next stitch on the left-hand needle to the right-hand needle as if to knit. Knit the following stitch on the left-hand needle. Place the left-hand needle into the second stitch on the right-hand needle and pass it over the first stitch on the right-hand needle—1 stitch decreased.

S(lip) S(lip) K(nit): This is a left-slanting decrease. Slip the next stitch on the left-hand needle to the right-hand needle as if to knit. Knit the following stitch on the left-hand needle. Place the left-hand needle into the second stitch on the right-hand needle and pass it over the first stitch on the right-hand needle—1 stitch decreased. (**Note** PSSO and SSK are interchangeable.)

Y(arn) O(ver): **When knitting the next stitch:** Bring the yarn in front as if to purl, then knit the next stitch. **When purling the next stitch:** Bring the yarn to the back of work as if to knit, then purl the next stitch. In both instances, you are creating an extra stitch and hole.

W(ith) Y(arn) I(n) B(ack): Bring the yarn to the back of the work and work the next stitch.

W(ith) Y(arn) I(n) F(ront): Bring the yarn to the front of the work and work the next stitch.

Yarn Substitution Guide

When substituting yarns, look for yarns that are the same weight and preferably the same fiber content as the yarn called for in the project. Then use the Craft Yarn Council of America chart as a guide.

If you want to substitute a yarn that does not have the same fiber content, for example, a cotton rather than the cashmere for the Big Sister's Sweater, the first step is do a gauge swatch. Does it match the required gauge, and does it give you the drape and feel that you want for that project? If so, use that yarn.

Take care to purchase the correct yardage amounts for the project. Every skein is different. One 50g ball may have 50 yd, while another has 250 yd. Always note the total yardage required of the pattern—and buy it all from the same dye lot!

GENERAL GUIDELINES FOR YARN WEIGHTS

The Craft Yarn Council of America has instituted a number system for knitting and crochet yarn gauges and recommended needle and hook sizes. The information provided below is intended as a guideline, and as always, swatching is key to being sure a chosen yarn is a good match for the intended project. More information can be found at www.yarnstandards.com.

CYCA	**1**	**2**	**3**	**4**	**5**
Yarn Weight	**SUPER FINE** Lace, Fingering, Sock	**FINE** Sport	**LIGHT** DK, Light Worsted	**MEDIUM** Worsted, Aran	**BULKY** Chunky
Avg. Knitted Gauge over 4" (10cm)	27-32 sts	23-26 sts	21-24 sts	16-20 sts	12-15 sts
Recommended Needle in US Size Range	1-3	3-5	5-7	7-9	9-11
Recommended Needle in Metric Size Range	2.25-3.25mm	3.25-3.75mm	3.75-4.5mm	4.5-5.5mm	5.5-8mm

Acknowledgments

As I finish up this manuscript, Cole is nearing his first birthday, and I must say, this been one of my best years ever. Thank you Rosy and everyone at Potter Craft for giving me the opportunity to write this book while enjoying my son's first year. Many days this summer were spent working in the dining room with Cole learning to crawl and playing with the dog under the table while Nora patiently played upstairs until I would take a break to go the park with all of them. I, of course, would bring along at least one knitting project!

This book was possible with the help of many, many friends who gladly knit sample projects, picked up shifts at the store, helped with color choices, posed for photos in woolen sweaters in Washington's August weather, and so much more. Thanks to Edyth Ferguson, Gina Polidoro, and Ricki Seidman for knitting beautiful samples; to Pierre, Eleanor, Elise, Aria, Cole, and Nora for posing for photos; to Peggy Greig for patiently checking and editing every project; to my in-laws for letting all of us invade the house to take these beautiful photos; and to Joe for taking beautiful photos.

A special thanks to my entire staff, who let me have this summer to work on the book and enjoy the kids. Thanks to Jessica for all your knitting and managing the stores. I would not have been able to do this without you. A warm thank-you to Olga, Donna, Maria, Amber, and Rachel for all your beautiful knitting.

Finally, a thank-you to my family: to my Mom for knitting some of the projects, to Nora for being patient with me this summer, and to my husband for not questioning my midnight-to-4-am knitting marathons. Thank you! Thank you! Thank you!

Project Resources

All supplies for the patterns in this book are widely available at fine yarn stores everywhere, including Stitch DC, in all three locations, or on the web at www.stitchdc. com. We've provided this listing of retailers and wholesalers to assist you in finding the closest supplier for the yarns used in this book. If you have trouble finding a product at the stores in your area, consult the websites listed to locate a distributor near you.

STITCH DC / CAPITOL HILL
731 8th Street SE
Washington, DC 20003
Phone: 202.544.8900

STITCH DC / GEORGETOWN
1071 Wisconsin Avenue NW
Washington, DC 20007
Phone: 202.333.KNIT (5648)

STITCH DC / CHEVY CHASE
5520 Connecticut Avenue NW
Washington, DC 20015
Phone: 202.237.8306

YARNS

ARTYARNS LUXURY HAND-
PAINTED YARNS
39 Westmoreland Avenue
White Plains, NY 10606
Phone: 914.428.0333
www.artyarns.com

BLUE SKY ALPACAS
PO Box 88
Cedar, MN 55011
Phone: 888.460.8862
www.blueskyalpacas.com

CLASSIC ELITE YARNS
122 Western Avenue
Lowell, MA 01851-1434
Phone: 978.453.2837
www.classiceliteyarns.com

DALE OF NORWAY
4750 Shelburne Road
Shelburne, VT 05482
Phone: 800.441.3253
www.dale.no

DEBBIE BLISS / KNITTING FEVER
PO Box 336
315 Bayview Avenue
Amityville, NY 11701
Phone: 516.546.3600
www.knittingfever.com

JADE SAPPHIRE
Phone: 866.857.3897
www.jadesapphire.com

KARABELLA YARNS
1201 Broadway
New York, NY 10001
Phone: 800.550.0898
www.karabellayarns.com

LORNA'S LACES HAND-DYED YARNS
4229 North Honore Street
Chicago, IL 60613
Phone: 773.935.3803
www.lornaslaces.net

MISSION FALLS
CNS Yarns c/o Milgram
156 Lawrence Paquette
Champlain, NY 12919
Phone: 877.244.1204
www.missionfalls.com

ONE WORLD BUTTON SUPPLY CO.
41 Union Square West, Suite 311
New York NY 10003
Phone: 212.691.1331
www.oneworldbuttons.com

PEAR TREE ORGANIC YARNS
PO Box 463 Torquay
Australia 3228 VIC
phone: 61 03 5261 6375
www.peartreeproducts.com.au

ROWAN / WESTMINISTER FIBERS,
INC.
US DISTRIBUTORS
165 Ledge Street
Nashua, NH 03060
Phone: 800.445.9276
www.knitrowan.com

THE PAPER SOURCE
Phone: 888.PAPER-11
www.paper-source.com

VERMONT ORGANIC FIBER
COMPANY
52 Seymour Street, Suite 8
Middlebury, VT 05753 USA
Phone: 802.388.1313
www.vtorganicfiber.com

Index

Page numbers in *italics* indicate illustrations.